# (al)ONE
# Thriving a Stroke

## STACIE BROEK

# DEDICATION

This book is dedicated to my village and to all of you who knew me when the only word I could mutter was "One."

# Table of Contents

"When you are this far down, the only way to go is up," said a clever woman, Florence Dunklee, the ultimate kick-ass-and-take-no-prisoners grandmother. I'll have what she's having.

(al)ONE

# INTRODUCTION

I am 46 years old and the only word I can say is "One."

This is a book about transformation. About my transformation. About something which should have broken me, but instead has become the glue that's fixing me.

I survived a stroke on 20 February 2019. I was young. I was a wife to a gregarious Dutch guy, a mother to three young children, a writer, and an aspiring artist. But I was also, unfortunately, oblivious.

Oblivious to the signs of stroke. I'm not afraid to admit that I thought I would die from a mishap—a devastating accident or adventure gone wrong. I always thought that it would be something beyond my control, at the hands of others. I was conceited and egotistical. Living through this stroke-hell caused by my own body left me unhinged. I came close to death, and I didn't find it scary. In fact, it felt tender and warm, like an embrace.

Oblivious to the agony that it wreaks on its survivors and their carers. In my most fragile state, with a catheter

1

and confined to my hospital bed, I was not focused on survival. My only thoughts were of connection. Hugging seemed paramount and the times in between my visitors seemed a lifetime. On the one hand, something about this was liberating. On the other hand, I struggled in the aftermath, not only with my relationships, my therapies, and my emotions, but also with myself.

And I was oblivious to its possibilities. The first year attempted to rip my heart out, trample on it and stuff it like waste in the bin. Before, I thought I knew what a bad day looked like. When I was driving, other people were always the idiots. I would silently chastise my husband for buying the wrong brand of tortillas or how he mowed the garden. I was smug, selfish and exhausting. I blamed others for a great many things. Now, I feel great shame when I yell at my children or scoff at a waitress.

This is my story of surviving the single most unrelenting, merciless, grim and horrific twelve months I have ever known, of the darkness and anguish that it provoked.

I want to share this story with you because I need you to understand, to give you a glimpse inside my mind. The mind of a survivor.

# CHAPTER 1
## Sex, Drugs and Rock & Roll (but not really)
*Before: I thought that my life was whole.*

My entire childhood was spent in the same house, in the same Pennsylvanian village. It was idyllic and full of memories. I spent my summer days swimming or playing in the woods with the neighborhood boys and summer nights catching fireflies and laying in the dewy grass trying like mad to figure out which of the tiny sparkles above was the North Star.

I was lucky enough to get my first job at the age of fifteen, as a lifeguard at my town's community swimming pool. I loved every minute of that freedom. The hours were hard, but the pay was great, especially as my bank account consisted of a few bucks from babysitting and the odd savings bond from my Aunt Lena.

Growing up I learned to shoot a gun, how to ride my bike as fast as it could go, and how to race my four-wheeler against a snowmobile. Come September, it was always back to school and football games cheering our team to the win.

It was a time before mobile phones, before the internet. I can remember wrapping the very long cord of the kitchen (rotary) phone around the corner so that I could have a private conversation in the next room. I think fondly of that time. We didn't know or care about tomorrow. We thought, as children do, that we were immortal.

I was friends with all the cliques: The burnouts. The jocks. The honor students. The pretty girls. I earned extra credit by volunteering to help kids with special needs and for a long time considered a teaching career. I was on the volleyball team, the ski club and the National Honor Society. I remember sleepless nights gossiping about secret crushes with my girlfriends, with flashlights casting creepy shadows on the wall.

I created memories and I remember having loads of fun times. But, I always spoke a different language from my family and friends in that Pennsylvania village. My goals were crazy to them and my ideas the same. I never really fit in in that small town. While my high school friends were dating and happily "teen-aging," I was focused on submitting early admissions applications to universities. They were bonding and growing up together; I was reading fashion magazines and dreaming of life outside the confines of small-town Pennsylvania.

By that time, you might say that I was ready to make my first change. Although I was blissfully unaware of the changes that were taking place inside my mind, I was dreaming of a place where nobody knew my name. You see, the feeling of entrapment was not something that I can bear easily; it still isn't. I saw my early entrance into university in 1990 not as an escape, as it was interpreted by my friends, but as a stepping stone to open my world.

# (al)ONE

What I didn't realize, as I drove off to college in a city two hours from my home, is that I would spend the better part of the next four years soaking up the culture of people who were like-minded. I found it exciting, but not enough to hold my interest. The real lure was getting my bachelor's degree and high-tailing it to New York, which I did as soon as I had enough credits to graduate, in 1993.

The ten years I spent in New York were complicated, and I quickly formed a love-hate relationship with the city. It challenged me in ways that I could not have imagined, encouraging me and pushing me forward while also exasperating and confusing me. As a city, it was accepting, yet fiercely demanding. I loved it.

In New York I found myself evolving into an adult. One that lived alone, owned a car and adroitly managed a career. I had never felt more alive. I thought that I would never leave that city. However, meeting Johan, my future husband, opened my world yet again and served as a catalyst for another change. Suddenly, my thoughts didn't only include New York and New Yorkers. They expanded to include this weird and wacky Dutch guy, who talked differently and thought differently and who had grown up all over Europe. My universe suddenly broadened, yet again.

You see, I am dichotomous. Change is not my usual go-to mode. I am a hard-core creature of comfort and revel in the known. It drives my husband mad that I can walk the exact same way to the shop each and every time I go. For me, there is no question about it: I will always take the same path, each and every time. I love the security of a good plan, even if it is only walking to buy milk. That's just me.

But change is somehow, weirdly, a deep and natural part of me too. Through all of the transitions in my life, I have also taken quite a few game-changing detours. When Johan had to relocate to London from New York in 2003, early on in our relationship, I didn't hesitate to follow. I was in! I packed up my independent self and dove head and heart first into our new life together.

It was undeniably the first time that I felt out of my league. Sure, I'd visited London plenty of times, but as we were packing up my tiny studio apartment in New York, where I'd laughed and cried about many boys, gotten my first new car (and a garage to keep it in), and found and rented my first summer beach place, I felt the panic creeping in. My life was already well-sorted! Why was I insistent on changing it?

I didn't like London. My New York attitude didn't serve me well there and I felt like an outsider. I was lucky that my firm transferred me when I gave notice that I was moving to London, but unlucky that now I was traveling all the time for work. As a marketing brand manager for my company's biggest licensed products, they loved the fact that I could grow the European business. So back and forth I traveled between the factories, the licensor, and my home in New York.

I loved my career and the freedom it gave me but, while Johan was rekindling his relationships with old mates, I was generally stuck in one hotel room or another. A year into this routine, after a long, arduous business trip from London, to LA, to Tokyo, to Hong Kong and back to London, I was done. I remember distinctly the day that I told Johan that I wanted to quit my job. It must have been a complete shocker for him. To this day, I am proud of myself to have stood my ground. I told my employer the next time I flew to New York.

I focused on planning our wedding, finding a new job, and building my London life. I hired a Dutch tutor to teach me the language. I started running again, meeting my mates for lunch, and falling in love with tennis.

In early 2005, I was focused on entrepreneurship, but that was precisely the time I was offered a job in Zürich; I think that it was just foreshadowing for what was yet to come. So, I aborted that mission and took the opportunity to pack up our London life and make a brand new start in Zürich, working as a Head of Marketing for Swarovski. The trouble is, and I can see this more clearly after my stroke, that I have always been on the hunt. For the next transition. For the next role. I was always on the lookout for the next big thing in my life, and it left me feeling exhausted. I never found comfort in myself, or just being myself.

In 2008, after a hard-fought battle to get pregnant, we gave birth to Lulu and Friso and two years after that, in 2010, I decided to end my corporate career. I took some time off, focused on getting pregnant again, taking trips with my young family and enjoyed the role of mother. Although I've never looked back, it's possible that I was searching for the fulfillment and the power that the office had provided me with. Once I had given birth to our third child, Cleo, two years later, my mind began to wander again. Was it enough? Did I want more? Did I expect more of myself and my life?

I sincerely didn't know the answers to these serious questions and this concerned me. Something was still missing. I knew that going back to a marketing job was not for me. Despite all of its glamor, I found it stifling. Entrepreneurship seemed like the best of both worlds, something to activate my mind, something to feel powerful and something to calm the voices churning in my head. I had many half-assed business plans but something inside of me was compelling me to take this option more seriously. After a year and a half and one failed business, I finally found my groove with a new friend and, later, business partner.

Throughout all of the game-changing roles I have played, moving from New York to London and eventually to Zürich, I experienced so many meaningful life events. I got engaged, married, had children, built my career, and started a business. It's only with hindsight that I can see that I was still evolving, searching for what makes me tick.

Our first years living in Switzerland were meaningful and memorable and our connections are very deep. We had our three children there, we built friendships and made a house a home.

At the end of 2016, Johan was offered a new position within his company and it came with an unusual and seductive opportunity for our family. The job was located in Japan, and our family of five would be sent from Switzerland on an international assignment to Tokyo. So, we jumped. We jumped fully and whole-heartedly.

Once we moved to Tokyo, Johan went to the office each day and I kept myself busy with loads of new activities. My newly found freedom enabled me to go explore with my camera in tow, to write with abandon, and to focus on my children in a new and deep way. I got busy with volunteering at the children's school. In fact that's exactly where I met Katja, who would later become a close friend, as we ran the school's annual charity event that year. When we weren't knee-deep in planning, then we were exploring, taking pictures and writing about it.

I will be the first to admit that my life was a little bit more "spoiled expat wife" than sex, drugs & rock-n-roll. I was still searching for something to sink my teeth into, although my creative side was screaming with pleasure at my new life. I was building a life that was intrinsically me, starting from the bottom and working my way up.

I look back at all of the roles I have played and I ask myself, which "me" am I proudest of? Why? What does that "me" look like and feel like? From where did she get energy? Am I still that "me?" Underneath it all, I believe that I have undergone a fundamental shift in the way that I see people and experiences.

On 20 February 2019, Stacie 1.0, that strong, feisty, independent, fire-eater of a girl gave way to a more inquisitive version of me, leaving me with these questions: "What would have happened if I didn't suffer my stroke?" and "How is it possible that I didn't do the work before?"

# CHAPTER 2
## The Crash
*Day 1: What would you do if it was your wife?*

My stroke happened on Wednesday, 20 February 2019. Just shy of two years living in Tokyo. At age forty-six. With no real cause for alarm.

I remember the morning clearly. I was getting ready to meet Katja for coffee, before we went off to the Parent Student Association meeting. Truth be told, I had not been feeling well for days. I didn't know what was wrong with me; I felt so tired and lethargic. It wasn't like me. My days were generally packed to the brim as I juggled three kids, a household and writing. I'm not talking about the general fatigue that goes with being a mom of three, making you collapse into bed at nine o'clock in the evening. This was more of a relentless, broken-down feeling of debilitation. And, it left me feeling hopeless.

I never made it to that meeting.

It's funny how we tell ourselves little lies when we don't know what's happening to our bodies. I've always been attuned to what's going on inside and I'm a massive self-advocate for getting to the bottom of any problems. I am doctor-friendly and never missed a chance for a massage or a chiropractic appointment. But with this situation, I just didn't see how anyone could help me. So, I just carried on with my jam-packed schedule.

On Monday, two days before my stroke, I gathered my tennis racket and hit the courts. I was pumped, or at least I was trying to convince myself that I was pumped. What I didn't know then that I know now, is that this tennis game might have been a sneaky culprit in provoking my stroke. As I raised my racket to the sky to hit a smash, the funniest thing started happening. I started seeing spots where the ball should be. Not just one or two spots—those little buggers were actually hiding the ball from my vision. My coach made me sit down on the bench for a moment, but I shrugged him off, insisting that my symptoms were simply due to the fact that I hadn't eaten enough for breakfast. Lie number one.

I went home and couldn't shake this sluggish, fuzzy feeling twirling around in my head. I remember thinking that if I could just have a nap, I would feel better. A deadline was looming and I had a bunch of writing to get done for it, so I carried on. I remember driving to the family club that evening, with my kids in the car. My principal goal was to let them do their activities, do their homework and feed them so I could finally lay down in bed.

As I awoke the next day, I felt nervous. Lulu and Friso were going off to ski camp with their school. I didn't have time to decipher if my unease was just jitters or the nagging malaise that was still affecting me. When I dropped the guys at school to meet the ski bus, I remember turning to my friend Gordana, another school mother, and saying, "I am just utterly tired."

She commiserated, telling me that she had said the exact same thing to her husband that very morning. We agreed that the winter months were doing our collective heads in and that was that.

After the drop-off and the goodbyes, I hit the courts with Katja. It was curious to see, but those strange spots were in my way again. It was beyond all reason. I had never dealt with something like this before. I just wanted them to vanish. I didn't make a fuss, but after popping some mints in my mouth and telling myself that it was just because I hadn't eaten enough for breakfast, I carried on exercising. Lie number two.

Afterwards, I could no longer ignore the fatigue, the weariness, that had enveloped my body. I convinced myself that taking a nap on the couch was all that I needed. Lie number three. I was fine after that nap. Lie number four.

That Wednesday morning, where one phase of my life ended and another, more complicated, tricky one, ended up taking its place, started out like any other day. Except it wasn't. I awoke with numbness in my lower right leg. The feeling of listlessness, inertia, was overtaking my being. Here I was, a forty-six-year-old woman, in good health and, yet, I was about to have a stroke.

I would like to say that, in this moment, running through my mind were my kids, my husband and the emergency number posted on the refrigerator, but actually what goes through your mind when you're knee-deep in having a stroke is nothingness. It is a state of bliss that takes your mind off of the here and now and redirects you and your thoughts to fairyland.

# (al)ONE

One minute I was asking Johan to take Cleo to the bus, while texting that I would be a little bit late, because I just needed to lay down, and the next moment I was looking at my phone, trying like mad to remember how the bloody thing worked and what I was trying to text anyway.

And then there was nothing.

As I relive the days leading up to my stroke, I am saddened by the thought of the what-ifs. What if I had gone to my doctor? What if I had been aware of the signs for stroke? Sadly, I'll never know the answers.

There are some memories which are seared into my brain like scars. When Johan found me, lying in a half-dressed state, phone in hand, he was incredulous, asking me the same questions over and over.

"Stacie, can you hear me?"

"Stacie, can you say something?"

"Stacie, what is the password for your phone?"

I knew that he was there and that he wanted me to answer those questions, but it really didn't register as important. I didn't realize the urgency. I remember the fear in Johan's voice, although it didn't alarm me. Later, I realized that in his state of shock, he was frantically trying to use my phone to call for help. Because he didn't know the code and he continued to push the numbers several times, he blocked the phone. To this day, I have suppressed my memory of that code.

I remember Katja's green sweater. I remember thinking I should tell her that it is a nice color on her. It didn't seem at all strange to see her in my bedroom. Katja's husband, Olivier, is a doctor. He was traveling on business the day of my stroke. Of course, Katja phoned him several times that day, but I will always remember her saying that, in the morning, she called him as we were waiting for the ambulance to arrive. She quickly described the scene that was unraveling in my bedroom. She asked, with desperation, "Is there anything that looks like a stroke, but isn't?" Olivier answered his wife that, sadly, there was not.

I remember waking up from my slumber as the paramedics were taking me down the stairs and again when the Emergency Room nurses were tugging my bracelets off of my wrist. Funnily enough, I remember sitting up and asking for a bar of soap. That got them talking, or rather questioning my perception of reality. Upon bringing me that bar of soap, I demonstrated how to rub it on my wrist, so that the bracelets would come off more easily.

I remember Johan telling me that I couldn't go home just yet because the doctors wanted to run some tests, an angiography. I felt my first anxious moments, because his face, which was normally so calm, had fear written all over it. My perception was slowly catching up to reality.

I remember waking up from my slumber in the operating theater to the kind faces of my husband and my best friend. They were sweetly telling me something which I have no recollection of, but they looked so tender, so loving. I just knew that everything was going to be ok.

I remember the insurmountable dread that I felt when I woke up during my surgery. I couldn't move because my head was in a vice. I couldn't talk to signal that I was awake. I just stared wide-eyed at the calmness of what seemed like a dozen surgeons staring at computer screens. And then nothing.

Those hours must have seemed like a lifetime for Katja and Johan. I truly can't imagine what they had to endure for those long and seemingly endless hours, all the while putting on their brave faces. For nearly ten hours, they waited. They didn't eat. Thankfully they had one another.

Johan had the crushing job of phoning my mother, who was laden with shock, worry and fright. Of course she wanted like hell to be there, grasping his hand as I went thru surgery. As she is located in the United States and I was in Japan, she had a taxing long few hours to spend from afar.

As she woke up my stepfather to tell him, her fears turned into something much bigger than simple emotion. It was like she felt the need to protect me, wrap me in her arms and kiss my cuts and scratches goodbye. I can only imagine what she was thinking, the need to shield me from the dangers of my own body, must have hurt like hell. She was patiently waiting for any news from Johan or Katja.

As it turned out, I had suffered a dissection (a tear) in my internal carotid artery, the artery which supplies blood to the brain. The normal treatment for this is a stent, a small mesh tube surgically implanted to reinforce the artery, but because my carotid artery is redundant (curly or torturous), it would make the surgery more difficult. As one can imagine, that was not something that you hear every day. Instead of letting the utter bewilderment that Johan must have been feeling pull him under, he went into survival mode. He forced himself to reach out to anyone and everyone who could shed some light on the situation.

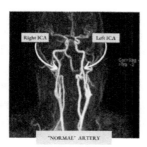

Scrolling through his internal Rolodex, he found a couple of people who he thought could help. He used his nervous energy to educate himself, talking to doctors and surgeons, anyone in his network of friends and colleagues who could help. Johan spoke at length with his father, a practical man of few words, who impressed on him that in all critical junctions, he should ask the neurosurgeons one question: "Would you do this if it was your wife?"

Johan is fierce in business and a not-too-serious, loads of fun Pappie, but tackling a personal problem of this magnitude, I can only imagine the agony, the internal battle that was consuming him.

At a certain moment, during my surgery, the doctors came to Johan and asked him whether or not they could use an experimental approach, because the conventional method was not working. That's where his logic and perseverance proved instrumental. He kept calm and used reason. As he had spent the last several hours on the phone with friends and his very level-headed father gathering information, he was prepared for the question.

"Would you do it if it was your wife?" he asked my surgeon.

"Yes," the doctor replied. "I would also do it if it was my daughter."

So Johan agreed.

And then, he was permitted to enter the surgery, with Katja, to see me before they began.

What goes through one's mind when making such a significant decision? How did my husband, with his spirited, lighthearted approach and his social butterfly way make this decision? What did it do to him and his psyche? On the operating table lay his partner. His wife. Mother to three. A daughter. A friend.

Of course it affected him. It makes me shudder and thank him all at once.

# (al)ONE

My operation was a success. As it turns out, this surgery had only been performed ten times in all of Japan. I got lucky.

# CHAPTER 3
## Picking Up Shattered Glass
*The Beginning of Week 1: Fight with integrity.*

When I awoke from my surgery many hours later to find that I was all on my own, dark, creepy blackness entered my thoughts.

I have the feeling that this blackness smelled. Like what, I really don't know. Maybe it was the cleanliness of a Japanese hospital or, perhaps, it was the fear that was welling up inside me.

I wanted to scream.

Was I laying on my hand? It felt like it was asleep.

I was alive, but the incessant urge to see Johan, who had gone home to get some sleep, was unbearable. I remember sobbing and sobbing for him. I must have scared the poor nurses to death. I couldn't talk, although at the time I didn't realize this. I couldn't move the entire right side of my body. I didn't know where I was or what was wrong with me.

So I panicked. I started screaming for someone, anyone. The kindest nurse stood over me and with her eyes told me to calm down, that she was in control, and while I had every reason to be scared, that it wouldn't help.

She then said something in Japanese to her colleague.

That detail is not insignificant. In fact, I didn't have any idea that this incomprehensible exchange would foreshadow the events of the next six weeks. That compassionate nurse was speaking to me with her eyes, because words failed us both on this occasion. Her, because she didn't speak English, and me, because as I would learn, I suffered a stroke.

Whatever she said to her colleague must have included instructions to call Johan, because like a flash he was there. I later learned that he was home, showering, and he actually missed that call. When he got out of the shower he picked up his phone and didn't know whose number it was, so he raced like mad to the hospital. He thought I had died.

Never in my life had I been so grateful to see Johan. Never. I was scared. I had no idea what had happened. But just seeing him made me want to crawl in his arms and block the rest out. I cannot even remember what he said or didn't say to me. It was as if that day came in pieces, like shattered glass.

I remember his smell. His touch. His worried eyes. The rest is a blur.

Looking back, I did not have the feeling that there was anybody else there but me in the room. Which was not the case, as I was in the Emergency ICU. From my vantage point, lying face up, it wasn't easy to judge. As I took in my surroundings, there seemed to be a gentle calmness to the room. I couldn't hear anything except for a faint buzzing and beeping. I imagined the nurses were the shadows humming in the distance, but through my contactless-eyes I could not be sure.

Only later—much later—would I understand what had happened to me.

Here's the thing: most people know the common causes of a stroke that relate to poor lifestyle decisions, such as heavy smoking, excessive drinking and bad diet. Or, something that happens to "old" people. And in fact, the majority of strokes do happen to people aged sixty-five and older.

My stroke was different. It was caused by a carotid artery dissection (CAD), an incredibly rare condition which was undetected until I was rushed to the hospital. A carotid artery dissection happens when the layers of the artery are spontaneously separated, or torn. This separation causes a pool of blood to form in the artery wall.

It is estimated that carotid artery dissections only happen to two in one-hundred-thousand people, or one-hundred-sixty-thousand people, per year (according to Dodds MD, Jodi A. *Carotid and Vertebral Artery Dissection: A Guide for Survivors and Their Loved Ones*). The causes of this infarction can be spontaneous. They can be due to injury. Some very common injuries, such as headbanging, going to the hair salon (tipping back in the chair for the wash) and playing sports with high contortion on the neck, such as tennis, can be the culprit.

Here's another little-known fact: only two to three percent of those that suffer a carotid artery dissection actually experience a stroke. This means that globally, each year, approximately four-thousand people have a stroke due to carotid artery dissection. The other one-hundred-fifty-six-thousand are either treated for their symptoms, i.e. blood thinners, or watched carefully until the blood is reabsorbed by the body.

I have always joked about my unluckiness and often laugh that "if it's going to happen to anyone, it will be me". While this seems like a cynical attitude, it's true that I am unlucky; I'm always stepping into dog poo, my house and car were broken into, falling pregnant took me many trials and tribulations–I've become used to expecting the unexpected. It is also true that I find luck within my unluckiness. In this case, my husband was at home. He recognized the signs of stroke. He called the ambulance. I was taken to the right hospital. A team of neurosurgeons were brought in and worked tirelessly for nearly ten hours, in a surgery that they had never performed. I was Japan's number eleven.

Suddenly, I found it less amusing to be one in two million people who survived a stroke this way, to be on this crappy side of luck. I ask myself: Could I have seen it coming? Why didn't I know the signs of stroke? What if I had truly been a self-advocating pit bull then? Could I have been more proactive when I saw the early warning signs of my carotid artery dissection? They were there, in hindsight, but I politely ignored them.

Fatigue that was incapacitating. Seeing spots when I was playing tennis the two days leading up to my stroke. The fact that I woke up with a "dead-leg" on the day of my stroke. In my case, my carotid artery dissection could have happened when I reached up to hit a smash, but sadly it wasn't detected early enough to catch my stroke. The pool of blood traveled to my brain.

It only struck me afterwards, as hindsight generally does, that I had been suffering gripping neck pain for over four months. Although this wasn't a sure sign of my stroke, as it was on the other side of my neck, I now kick myself for not being aggressive enough to find out what this pain was, for not being proactive. I might have guessed that the fatigue was a sign that my brain was on overload, but the other symptoms—seeing spots and waking up with a dead leg—left me in wonderment. What if I had taken the earlier warning signs seriously?

As I lay there with neurologists and medics all rushing around, I couldn't have known what it meant for my future. I just wanted Katja and Johan to sit by me, as I was in and out of consciousness. They made me feel comfortable, in the purely selfish, self-centered and narcissistic way that you act when you are on holiday. No cares in the world. The world was reduced to me and the two people sitting, sometimes together, sometimes separately, at my bedside. If they weren't there I immediately felt scared.

It didn't occur to me in those first few days to wonder where my children were. I find this extremely absurd. I spent the better part of eleven years taking care of them and it didn't even dawn on me where the hell they were. I can recall the doctors asking me to recite my children's names, in an effort to gauge my cognitive abilities. I didn't know them. I couldn't say them, even if I did. So the whole exercise seemed, in my view, ridiculous. I knew that I had children, but the fact somehow seemed unimportant. It just didn't register.

So, I spent my time waiting. For Johan. For Katja. For the nurses.

Of course, Johan's world was completely crashing down around him, but all I saw was the man I married coming and going. Coming and going. The adjustment being all of a sudden alone, to having a sick wife in Japan and three children to look after, could have brought a grown man to his knees. However, communicating this to my friends and our children was more than he could grapple with.

He recently told me that when he called my dear friend Maria, he accidently called via Facetime video. As she picked up and he realized he'd started a video call, he immediately hung up. You see, she had a way of getting deep inside you, picking apart your thoughts and your intentions like no other. The last thing that he was prepared for was looking into her soulful, dark brown eyes and telling her that her friend had suffered a stroke, a hundred million miles away.

As he fumbled to call her back without video, Maria was quicker. She got him in front of her, with the camera. As soon as he was face to face with her, he just broke down. He felt paralyzed and unable to control the regret of telling my best friend, the strongest woman that we have ever known, what had happened.

Maria is no stranger to pain, suffering and sickness. As a stage four ovarian cancer survivor and advocate for nearly eleven years, she knew that something was very wrong. As she, with her calm and rational manner, plucked the words from Johan, she asked questions to understand the situation and let him off the line. She was levelheaded and sensible, making Johan's job easier with her empathy.

While I was struggling to remember that I had children, Johan was preparing to tell them about my stroke. As he and Katja collected the children from school, after their ski camp and three short days after my stroke, he felt that his world collapsed. He was so shaken up that he drove the wrong way home. In his own words, he was gormless. He lacked sensibility, only focusing on the enormous task at hand.

Luckily for him, he wasn't alone. He had help. Katja was there, by his side, through it all. Katja, although we had known each other for less than one and a half years, along with her husband Olivier and their three awesome children, stepped in as they'd do for their own family. There was no question about it. No hesitation.

Katja slid into a role which was much more than a friend. Much more than a sister. In Katja, I had found a kinship of the mind and will. We found ourselves inextricably intertwined for this difficult journey that we call life.

As he gathered the children on the couch, the endless questions of "where is mommy" about to do his head in, he silently went over his speech one more time. The children were there, looking to him for an explanation. So, slowly he began and stumbled. He began again. He had trouble finding his words.

If you had met Johan on the street in the days or weeks following my stroke and asked him about me, he would have not been able to get the word "stroke" out. It was a mental block, a sort of protection against his suffering.

However, he'd prepared for this and as he willed himself to spit out the words, he knew that there were three little souls hanging on to his every syllable. So, he began with a straightforward statement: "Mommy had a stroke. She is in the hospital." I can only imagine what everyone was thinking or feeling at the time. Johan had to stop, to catch his breath, to make the room stop spinning, and Olivier took over.

Afterwards, Katja cooked dinner for all of them, our collective six children and our "wives" as we sarcastically, albeit lovingly, call our husbands, while the kids were playing video games or watching movies. It was the first time that Johan had all of the kids home without me.

I cannot imagine what they were feeling, how they adjusted to life when it seemed unfair or perplexing in the most confusing way possible. What does such news do to a child? Can they even process it?

I asked them, not too long ago, how they felt when Pappie told them about my stroke. Friso gave it a thought, and responded in the most natural way that it "felt weird." They just heard awful news about me and there they were, playing like normal. In answering my question, he appeared uncomfortable, as if I might be upset with his honesty. Lulu could not or did not want to answer.

That is the incredible mystery of humans. We are so complex. We have this massive toolbox of weapons to either deal with the pain or to shut it out completely.

Katja stayed past supper, cleaned the dishes, and tucked my three into their beds. We were in this together: the first wives club and our broods.

It's said that a stroke brings you back to infancy in some ways. There I was, a very outspoken forty-six-year-old woman with three children, a prior Head of Marketing, business owner and blogger, reduced to a needy lump. I had a catheter, I couldn't walk, I couldn't talk, and I was unaware of it all.

I'll never forget a few weeks afterwards, my mother was reading one stroke survivor's book to me. I couldn't read it myself. The author said in her book that she knew from the time that she woke up from her stroke that she was going to fight. That she had to fight for herself. She was self-aware enough to have this thought. I was enraged when my mother read this to me. How could this woman say that? I was like a newborn and she was ready to fight?

My world was shattered by this concept. I thought that I had done something wrong, that my behavior at this juncture was not correct. It made me feel inferior. I'd always been a person who saw things black or white, and to me, this was no different. Either I was following in her footsteps to recovery or I was never going to get better. End of chat.

This survivor's tale was my lifeline at the time. I knew in my heart and soul that I could and would make myself better just as she had done. She had been my superhero and her book my bible, up until that point. I couldn't yet distinguish that all strokes and stroke survivors are different and that her reality might be far different from mine. At that time, as I stopped my mother from reading that horrible, blasphemous book to me, I didn't have any such realizations.

My basic needs were being met, so much like an infant, I found myself napping and waking up. Napping and waking up. I didn't have the will, the foresight or the inclination to resist.

It didn't dawn on me here and now that I could fight. That I wanted to. That it was even an option. The impact of being a forty-six-year-old stroke survivor meant, to me, that I was now seeing every situation, every moment, through the fog of this new reality. I knew I had children, but they didn't register as important. I knew I could not feel my right side, but the consequences of this were lost on me. It's like I was seeing everything through a dull window of existence, only breathing air in and pushing it back out.

I am a fighter. I take it for granted, this fighting spirit. I have a survivor mentality. However, during those first few days, it was only seeing Johan and Katja, those who provided me with an emotional womb, a nest to cuddle up in, that got me through.

I would like to think that in my first few days I made up my mind to fight, and in some subconscious ways perhaps I did. Perhaps your true spirit comes to the surface when you are brought back to your most basic state. Or perhaps it was my mother reading that book to me. Even so, I was oblivious to what lay ahead.

# (al)ONE

I was lucky enough to be with Maria just before she passed. She told me, "I have lost the fight. Continue fighting, Stacie, for us all. Fight with integrity."

I am prepared to do exactly that, my friend.

# CHAPTER 4
## Channeling My Inner Pit Bull
*The End of Week 1: Fighting my way through the rubble my life had become.*

The doctors had predicted that I would spend two weeks in the ICU and then be strong enough to move out to a ward with less supervision from the nurses and doctors, where I would spend another four to six weeks. They sent plenty of doctors and therapists to my bedside through those first couple of days.

I remember some of them. I remember the psychologist who asked where I was from. She seemed nice enough and I felt happy to see her again.

I remember the physiotherapist who entered the room. She was quiet. I could sense that she was tough, yet soft. As she smiled at me, she asked if she could touch my leg. I politely gave her permission. After moving it around and around she persisted. She wanted me to sit on the edge of my bed and swing my legs around. I thought I could trust her. So, I did what she asked me to do. She then asked me to hold the bars of the bed and to stand up.

I don't know where I got the courage to follow her orders. Looking back, I thought she was half crazy. Perhaps that's what made me do it. It was surreal. I could only feel half of my body. I had to look to believe that I was standing. I really was! Such joy filled my heart.

It was the first time that I felt anything besides scared in those first few days.

Over time, I have come to realize that that physiotherapist bolstered my confidence and disallowed me to see the true state that I was in. Her assessment did not matter to me. I was blind to the fact that I was forced to have someone wheel me around like a newborn for the next few weeks. While I was glowing with a sense of accomplishment, she must have thought differently, that I was unstable and needed to gain strength and balance. However, what she did for my spirit was like an awakening.

Following my standing-up escapade, I became laser-focused on showering and using the toilet. My hair was in knots and the thought of my waste in a bag on the side of my bed was bothersome, to say the least. I was obsessed with these new goals. I hadn't eaten in two days. I couldn't move the right side of my body. I couldn't talk. Yet, this became very visceral to me, engrained deeply in my bones. I could not let it go.

I'm not known for my patience, and without a voice, I started a subconscious campaign to get the catheter out and to shower myself. I've never been a follower, but I wasn't aware of how deeply that was rooted inside me. If you take a moment to consider your most basic instincts, what are they? I would like to think that compassion and kindness are a couple of mine, but when I was reduced to my basic self, my infant-self, it was not the case at all.

Instead, my inner-pit bull took over.

I saw the need to have a shower and to go to the toilet and I was not going to settle for less. The next step in my recovery, although I didn't see it clearly then, was right there, calling out to me. If I could just wash my hair then I would feel human. If I could just use the toilet then I would not feel so sickly. These little voices were instinctual and it was useless to try to quiet them. I wasn't cognizant of it then, but the persuasive power of my mind to heal that which was broken beyond recognition was absolute. Once I provoked my brain with feelings of filth and feebleness, I gave myself the gift of possibility.

Within four days, my body had actually transformed. I was strong enough to leave the ICU and allowed to go to the twelfth floor, which had a private room just for me. The doctors were astounded by my progress. They had rarely seen such a rapid improvement from a stroke survivor in my condition. My body changed on a cellular level, allowing me to go off the catheter and to be brought to the bathroom. While I knew that I was a strong, healthy woman (who took her children camping without their papa, ran an events business lugging props and crates around and played tennis two to three times a week) being taken care of by some of Tokyo's best neurosurgeons, my determined belief and my blindness towards my limitations were crucial.

The twelfth floor seemed like a mystery to me. It was like we were transported to another world, one where it was just us, me and the nurse rolling me along. It resembled a ghost town. I distinctly remember the feeling I was all alone. *Were we even supposed to be there?* I remember asking myself silently.

Where was the beeping, the nurses buzzing around? I've never spent much time in hospitals but coming from the

ICU ward, this floor seemed like something from outer space. I didn't have the safe, secure feeling like I did in the ICU ward. How was I supposed to find my room? Would my family find me? I felt lost and frightened. I had heard Johan speak to the doctors about the twelfth floor. From my bed in the ICU it seemed like a dream, a private room all to myself.

It was so big, the maze of hallways and lifts. I began to feel disoriented, and a slight dose of paranoia settled in. Could I trust the nurses? Is this where they kept the foreign patients? I couldn't understand a single word that they were saying and this left me with a foreboding feeling. I was rolled to the last room in the right hand side of the hall. Or maybe it was the left? I felt utterly confused and panicky.

I was spinning and it seemed that there was no way to get control. It was the first time (of many more) I would experience this dominating urge, this all-consuming spiraling thought pattern of self-destruction. It was all or nothing for my brain and, due to my stroke, I had little control.

Just then, Katja arrived. She cruised down the hall and immediately began cracking jokes (which only she and I found funny). She made me temporarily forget and, much like an infant, my attention was shifted to a more positive place. The truth is that at that time I needed her to anchor me, though I was unaware of this.

I entered my room expecting to feel safe there but the door kept opening and re-opening with nurses and doctors and therapists coming through, all wanting to politely play their part in admitting me. The infinite barrage of questions that was asked of me, just four days after surviving a stroke, was mind-blowing. Or maybe in my diminished state it just felt that way? In my reduced capacity, I just didn't have the patience to deal with it. I was so tired. When would they leave me alone? I felt stuck between wanting to be a good student and my natural propensity to shine, and wanting it all to go away.

They were not speaking their own native language and so the process went very slowly. They would have to translate words from Japanese to English, which meant by the time they got to finish their sentence, I had forgotten most of it. What were they trying to ask? I really tried to find a meaning behind their questions, so they would leave me alone.

Even when I understood what they were asking me, I couldn't find an answer. Try as I might, I just could not find the words. What was blocking me? As I reached deep inside my brain for something which resembled words, it just registered blank in my mind. Even if I could understand the questions and if I could think of a suitable answer, I couldn't form the words.

As I would later find out, I was suffering from nonfluent aphasia, a condition which I'd never heard of before. Aphasia is simply defined as a common consequence of brain injury that negatively impairs your ability to communicate. However, the impacts of battling aphasia every single day are debilitating. I felt like I was either losing my mind or was gently being nudged to the point of mental exasperation. Aphasia causes a sudden, utter bewilderment. *How can I face the world?* I kept thinking.

It was a daunting blow for someone who had been a writer, a mama, and someone efficient at conveying their thoughts. I can remember being perplexed. It was like having a perpetual word on the tip of my tongue, always. Johan and Katja still joke about this, that after my surgery the only word I could speak was "one." You could have asked me my husband's name and I would promptly answer "one." Or my lunch order: "One." You see, I thought I was saying "Johan" or "soup, please" but actually all that was coming out of my mouth was either gobbledygook or "one." Perhaps that sounds crazy, them all laughing about my suffering. At the time, it wasn't at all funny. Johan and Katja didn't know if I would get better and I was completely unaware of the problem.

I was an exhausted heap that afternoon.

In an attempt to help me with articulating my thoughts, Katja made me a communication chart. We had a whale of a time making it, and I loved her for trying.

| WHEN | WHERE | WHAT | WHY |
|---|---|---|---|
| I | you | KIDS | JOHAN |
| VISIT | CALL | LULU | FRISO |
| CLEO | SCHOOL | SPORTS | FRIENDS |
| TRUTH | FUN | ICE PILLOW | HOT |
| COLD | THIRSTY | HUNGRY | IPAD |
| PHOTO | TOILET | VISIT | MOM |
| YES | NO | MAYBE | A LITTLE |
| COME | LEAVE | ASK | DOKTOR |
| NAP | HATE | SAD | SCARED |
| GOOD | GREAT | NOT GOOD | HORRIBLE |
| WHO | | | |

The night nurse that I had on the first night was a godsend. He had a better grasp of English than his colleagues and he tried his best to make me feel comfortable. He took his time with me, spoke gently, and tried to communicate. Throughout those six weeks, he would easily become my favorite nurse.

I didn't have any problems sleeping through the night. In fact, with the hum of my IV and the fact that every so often a nurse would come check on me, it felt safe. I felt safe in the hospital.

That first morning on the twelfth floor, Sunday, my children were allowed to come visit me for the first time. I was hyper-focused on getting a shower before they came. I needed, very selfishly, to present a strong, unbroken image to my three. I thought that if I could just shower and blow dry my hair, I could hide the fact that I didn't feel like the woman I was one week ago. I felt like a mute imposter with dirty hair, hooked-up to machines.

What they would see and experience only crossed my mind from my slanted, self-absorbed perspective. I wasn't capable of seeing it from their small eyes looking upwards. I was a drooling mess and couldn't speak. In some ways, I wasn't their mother anymore.

So I pushed the button to call the nurse.

How could I manage to make myself understood? I could not simply walk to the shower and explain what I wanted. I could not speak. I could not walk. When the nurse appeared I began gesturing with my hands. She acted as if she wanted to help, but couldn't figure out what I wanted. In the end, when she left my room, I was deflated. I couldn't possibly see my children like this!

I was just about to cause a small riot, when I saw the sweetest sight. The nurse from the ICU ward entered my room with a chair and walker. She was going to shower me. As she pulled my gown off and temporarily unhooked me from the machine, she made me feel as relaxed and as unselfconscious as I possibly could have been.

I am not ashamed to say that this was one of the best showers of my life.

When my children entered the hospital room, after being separated for days and a near-death experience, you would think that I would wrap them tightly in my arms to pacify them. One would think that, as a mother, I would do my best to shield them from the pain that they were undoubtedly feeling. But I couldn't. I couldn't act like a mother to my sweet babies and I didn't even realize it.

It was like my stroke had disabled me from feeling empathy. I wasn't concerned with how ski camp was or that I missed a few days of mommy-and-Cleo time. I only had *me* on my mind. Did I do it right? Was I presenting myself correctly? Did I get the reactions that I was seeking? Me. Me. Me.

I was nervous, not for my children, but for myself, in a self-absorbed, narcissistic way that I would have disliked if I could have seen it. Reduced to my most basic primal self, I was acting like an infant. I could not do anything to prevent this appalling behavior, as my emotional state was a direct result from surviving the stroke. So, instead of worrying about the IV attached to my arm or my children's reaction to it, I was purely focused on me.

The fact is that my children suffered my stroke along with me.

At the time, Lulu and Friso were that in-between, rascally age of 11 where you sit on the fence of adolescence, waiting for hugs from your mama and simultaneously too cool to receive them; and Cleo (the Squidge) was at the tender age of 6, my baby girl, whose life revolved around fairies, eating pasta with butter, and me, her mommy.

Nothing prepares an innocent child for the day when their mother suddenly turns from a super-hero into a normal, everyday human. When calamity strikes, children are left fully exposed. They can't shield themselves as we adults do.

As adults, we have spent our entire lives building intricate defense systems and putting them in place. We know how to block and bury our pain. We are experts at assigning blame or perhaps turning the whole kit-and-kaboodle over to a higher power, completely absolving ourselves. We have the authority to handle it any way we see fit. It is not always healing and it sometimes gets messy, but we have the power to affect our situation. We each have strategies for handling our pain.

Sitting there, shell-shocked, were my three, and try as I might, I could not act as their mommy. If you were observing us, like a fly on the wall, you would have seen a family in complete distress. It was a profoundly sad situation. The conversation was forced. I couldn't communicate verbally, so I was becoming frustrated with my inability to get my point across. Friso was trying like hell to understand me; he got it right more than a few times.

We were tip-toeing around each other as if we had just met one another. Our nerves were standing on end. I was in my bed and Cleo, perched on Johan's lap and as far away from me as she could get, could not help herself from staring at me. I beckoned her to come to me and, hesitantly, she came. Through a six-year-old's eyes, I should have seen that she was scared and looking for me to comfort her. But I couldn't. So, she immediately went into self-protection mode. She started, nervously, to chatter about something, anything, that could lighten the moment.

We were all skittish. With Cleo's chatter and Friso's compassion, I didn't know how to handle Lulu, who was sitting on the couch emulating a statue. If I had my wits about me, if I hadn't just suffered a stroke, it would be glaringly obvious that Lulu is my onion. She can hold layers and layers of pain, curled up in a tight ball, and never, ever, let it go.

It was like playing a game of peek-a-boo with her and I could feel my frustration bubbling up. I just wanted her to talk. Damn it! I couldn't get my words out! Failure and dissatisfaction, bordering on resentment, filled the air. I was going to blow.

Just then, Johan took Lulu outside the room. He was trying to coax her to let her feelings out. That it was ok to be afraid. But it didn't work. My poor little onion.

Luckily, my mother dropped everything when Johan called her the afternoon of my stroke. After my surgery, she wasn't going to trust anyone, not even my husband, to update her. She was my mother. And she needed to see me for herself. She arrived at my bedside on Tuesday, traveling all the way to Tokyo on her own from her holiday in Florida. Bless her, she went through a lot of hoops to make that trip possible, from having her passport overnighted from her home in Pennsylvania to booking the wrong dates with the airline.

My mother, Kay, became our crutch. We were all in desperate need of mothering. She has this ability to make everything seem natural. Like it was a typical Tuesday when she breezed into the hospital room, untouched by her nearly 24-hour trip to see for herself her daughter who just survived a stroke. Inside, of course, she was longing to put herself in my place. Hiding her broken heart, she arrived and enveloped us in her magic.

During the day she would see the children off to school, reassuring them that she would be there when they came back, and then she zipped to the hospital to spend the days with me. At night, when I was all tucked in, she raced back and had a glass of wine with Johan.

Looking back, no one really knew what they were doing. Johan was exhausted, just keeping his head above water. Barely. Well-meaning friends, who had heard the news through the grapevine, sent him messages. The best messages were ones of love and hope, not demanding that he respond. Kara, my dear Kara, was so good at that. You see, in this fragile state, he couldn't keep up with his life and the rate at which everything was happening to him.

Consequently Michiel, his best mate in Holland, took charge of updating everyone. He requested that all messages and questions for Johan were fielded through him. Even Marieke, Johan's beloved sister, never called. She patiently waited for an update through their parents.

There were some people, however, who just didn't get the message and depleted Johan's resources completely. There was one person, who I was very close to, who did just that. She called him repeatedly, requesting updates on my status. Because he was caught in the thick of it, Johan couldn't see the forest for the trees. He took each call, although it was very costly on his precious stamina.

All of a sudden, we were surrounded by could-have and would-have scenarios. We were living in a state of what-ifs. We knew we had dodged a bullet and we kept hugging each other, repeatedly. But I felt lost without him when he would leave the hospital. I felt lonely when he was gone. I was needy.

Practical things didn't mean the same as they did one week ago. We were just treading water through these days, with the help of my mother and Katja. The fear and uncertainty of being in Japan during the most difficult period of my life should have filled me with dread. The realizations that would follow in the coming weeks were excruciating. I found myself running from ghosts that I didn't even know existed.

Although I was completely naive about what the hell I was in for or what the hell it would entail, so far, I had found the courage and the strength to survive.

# CHAPTER 5
## Outwardly Lost
*Week 2: Was it so easy to replace me?*

We, as adults, have created this concept that to feel no pain is a good thing and something is wrong if we do. Rarely do we allow ourselves the space and the time that it truly takes to overcome our afflictions.

On the unlikely chance that we allow ourselves to find out which bits of the broken glass are worth being collected, those which were not shattered beyond recognition and those which were not broken in the first place, we can start to slowly accept our loss. The knowledge and craftsmanship to glue those broken bits into something whole again, acknowledging those that needed mending before, and the wisdom to accept the missing pieces, helps us to slowly rebuild.

I was unaware of everything that was afflicting me. My stroke left me unaware of the damages that it had caused. For the moment, as long as my basic needs were being met, I was complacent. It was a dull, sheltered existence by all means, but life outside of my hospital room didn't mean a thing to me. In my ignorance, Johan kept saying that I needed a speech and language therapist. I didn't understand why. Surely my communication skills would come back? I shrugged the suggestion off.

It was a tranquil period, the calm before the storm of realization that would soon follow. If I wanted to sleep, I slept. There wasn't any question. I didn't have to grant myself permission to take a nap, or several naps, throughout the day. I was peaceful and at peace.

Much like a baby, I was free to focus on anything and everything that I found pleasant. It was the polar opposite to how I lived before my stroke. Being content was easy. My hospital room was decorated with things that made me happy. My pillow from home, fresh flowers, my own bathrobe and slippers were my protection from evil. I felt comfort with these small things.

Random things, like my pill box, caused anxious feelings. It was too difficult to unwrap the pills with one hand; often I tried anyway and felt completely stressed by my difficulties. I remember feeling that it was humiliating to have one of those pill boxes that "old" people have with *Breakfast, Lunch* and *Dinner* written on it. Each time a nurse would come into my room, she or he would ask if I had taken my pills. In my mind, I thought they were crazy-hysterical about it and the question caused me to feel very tense. I had no perception, no appreciation, that these pills were important, that the anticoagulants and statins they contained could mean a matter of life or death.

From my vague, cushioned viewpoint, I couldn't comprehend all that was affecting me. As I would later come to understand, the list of my afflictions was much more extensive than simple communication problems. They included:

- Nonfluent aphasia (I could understand what was said to me, but I couldn't communicate back)
- Agraphia (I lost my ability to write)
- Impaired receptive language skills affecting:
    o Verbal
    o Written
- Emotional regulation disorder (My barometer to control my feelings was broken and I often felt too high or too low at any given moment)
- Impaired cognitive functions
    o Short-term memory impairment
    o Reduced attention
    o Impaired planning and organization
    o Impaired problem-solving skills
- Sensory integration disorder
    o Complete lack of sensation on my right side
- Right-sided hemiparesis (an inability to move or significant weakness on the right side of my body) affecting:
    o Fine motor skills (such as my grip and manipulation of objects within my grasp - I couldn't hold a fork or button my shirt)
    o Gross motor skills

There was a disconnect between my brain and my muscles so things like standing or lifting took me extra time, if I could do at all. My balance, coordination, body awareness, physical strength, reaction time and hand-eye coordination all were affected and damaged.

Two times per day, a nurse would come fetch me with a wheelchair and cart me off to physical therapy, where I would work on gross motor skills like walking, and occupational therapy, where I would use my hand to practice my fine motor skills by grabbing pegs and moving them correctly around a board. They would roll me down to the fourth floor and leave me standing in a line for my therapist. I did notice that I was much younger than the other patients who were lined up beside my wheelchair, but this fact meant nothing to me at the time. I don't know if it was the language barrier or my inability to speak, but the two times that I was faced with someone my age, probably because they had had an accident, it didn't dawn on me to speak with them. I found it healing to work like this and, in fact, it made me feel special. I had taken care of my three children for years, and to receive all this attention seemed wonderful.

Every day I was also visited by a therapist who would work on my hemifacial paresis. I don't know why, but I had to struggle to be nice to that man. In fact, I was often mean. He would come with a mirror and lead me through several exercises meant to restore sensation to my right side. I was supposed to look at my reflection in the mirror, while following along with his stupid exercises. I even chased him out of my room several times. I was being a bitch, but I didn't care. I knew that my face had changed and, perhaps, I didn't want to deal with this. Just the same, I can remember practicing those exercises in front of the mirror by myself, after brushing my teeth every night.

Johan, again using his amazing internal Rolodex, got straight to work to find me a speech therapist. He began firing off emails to people in multiple continents, advising them of our situation and seeking their advice on a speech therapist who could help me in Tokyo.

I have never met anyone with as many friends as my dear Johan has. Countless friends. In every country. From all walks of life. If I'm being honest, sometimes I get annoyed by his friends-in-every-corner style. However, this time, I was grateful because those emails to anyone and everyone pointed us to Seth. Seth, an American speech and language therapist located in Vietnam, actually came recommended by two people, Johan's Dutch ex-girlfriend and his English best friend's sister. What a small world.

Just short of two weeks after I suffered my stroke, we found Seth, had our first video call with him, and hired him on the spot. Johan told Seth that I am a writer and an avid reader who desperately needed those skills back.

So, Seth and I began to work together. Slowly. Getting to know and trust one another. One word at a time. We spent two hours together every day. Seth didn't mind that I could only manage to say or to write two words per hour. We focused on conversation, reading and writing. All of it was exhausting and brutally challenging for me, but with Seth's compassionate manner, I felt encouraged and reassured. He made sense in an otherwise foreign world of big, dark, scary creatures that I was beginning to believe actually existed.

I cannot explain how it feels to not know your own full name. Your address. Your children's birthdays. Their names. It cast doubt in the most insidious manner. It was menacing and dangerous. To aid me in recovering the words, I worked many hours with Seth on my "Automatic Speech."

Taken directly from my computer:
1) Stacie Broek

a)   Arrow Plaza Hiroo, #201, 2-17-21 Hiroo,
     Shibuya-Ku, Tokyo, Japan 1 5 0(zero) - 0 0
     1 2
One five zero - zero zero one two
    b)   Zero eight zero  8490 2494
    c)   Taxi: Hiroo Nisseki Dori
    d)   14 September 1972
2)   Johan Broek, 30 June 1968
3)   Lulu Broek, 14 February 2008
4)   Friso Broek, 14 February 2008
5)   Cleo Broek, 28   twenty eighth February 2012
     twelve
6)   Twenty eighth, February, two thousand and twelve

Recovering this information was a painfully slow
process. To be honest, I still have trouble remembering my
children's names even today. I easily confuse them with
Johan's name and each other. It is, to this day, a source of
pain for me. I loved naming our children. Johan and I each
attached our ten best baby names on the refrigerator and,
each day, we were allowed to put one at the bottom and
bring another up to the top. We went through this process
the better part of nine months.

I still cannot remember them.

I maintain that the stress of trying to remember them
hourly, like a performing monkey, each time the doctors
wanted to gauge my condition, caused me to collapse the
memory of their names. I regret this.

From my very protected perspective, everything was
brand new. Every sound was frightening. Every voice
caused me to jump. Each day would bring a new realization
of something that I used to do, think or say. It was
pleasurable and scary all at once. But I thought that as long

as I stayed in my shell, poking my head out here and there, I could manage.

Very slowly, I grew impatient with the nurses taking me down to physiotherapy (PT) and occupational therapy (OT) two times per day. Part of the problem was the time involved. They had to fetch me fifteen minutes prior to my appointment and then make me sit in the line. While I knew somewhere deep in my brain that I couldn't muster the strength to do it myself, I also knew that sitting and waiting was a waste of time. My compulsion grew into a full-blown obsession. I needed to go to my therapies alone. I have legs! They used to carry me wherever I wanted to go! I hated being carted around in a wheelchair.

Over the course of the next few weeks I had one vision. I was intensely focused, to the possible detriment to everything else, on walking myself to the elevator and taking it eight floors down to my therapies. It became my goal. I would practice day and night, standing up and holding my balance. When I could stand up, I would use anything to stabilize myself, my mom, my IV stand, the railing in the hallway.

As I built up my endurance, I managed to walk down the hall. Then to the nurses' station. And eventually I could even make a loop around the nurses' station. It was then that I found my new favorite place. I called it the sun room. It was actually the twelfth-floor lobby, but it felt like a slice of sunshine in an otherwise gloomy setting.

I was a patient. I was scared. And I believed that if I did everything correctly I would "pass." That if I followed the rules, then I would get a gold star for my performance. The full gravity of my situation had yet to dawn on me.

While I was barely clinging on, Katja had everything all under control. Or, at least it seemed that way from my very limited point of view. Her support and hands-on practicality were immeasurable. It must have been rough for her, managing two families, all the while visiting me every day in the hospital. Still, she would laugh and joke, making me feel like myself again.

I don't know how it happens that someone that you've met less than two years prior jumps in without a warning and makes it okay. Someone who sees what needs to be done and leaves no stone unturned to make it happen.

Katja organized someone to cook each night for my family. She made sure to check in with each one of my children every day before and after school. She gave the kids the feeling that she was always there for them. All the while giving me the same feeling. At the time, I didn't question this. But looking back, I am amazed; how did she do this? It's like she was everywhere at the same time and I definitely took it for granted.

Sometimes, my appreciation would wane. I would start to feel jealousy creeping up. It was hard watching her move through my life. With the children. With Johan. With the Parent Student Association projects. She seemed so efficient. And she was. She made it possible for all of us to get through the most desperate time in our lives.

Suffering a stroke means that your emotional regulation is compromised. I didn't really understand this; at the time, I just felt hurt and confused. I felt as if I was just treading water. In place. The same place. Every day.

Since that time, I've read that the effects of aphasia impact a survivor's quality of life more negatively than both cancer and Alzheimer's disease. Amazing. The inability to communicate with my friends, my family or my doctors was crippling, to say the least. What was actually happening to me would take me months, or even years, to understand. To this day, I have to work hard on regulating my emotional response.

At the end of the week Cleo (the Squidge) was performing at the school's assembly and having her birthday party. Not being able to watch your child perform on stage for the first time is heartbreaking. Not being with your daughter as she celebrates her seventh birthday is gut-wrenching. I could not be there to play games, eat cake, or watch her open her birthday presents. I could not congratulate her on a job well-done after her performance. My inability to be there for her during this time caused a well of emotions, slowly growing inside me like a cancer. I felt profoundly sad.

I could have sent my mother as a replacement, and I did to the school assembly, but I was too selfish to do it for Cleo's birthday party. I needed her there, with me, commiserating on my shitty luck. I was wallowing in self-pity and wracked with guilt. In like manner, Cleo started acting out at the end of the week. Perhaps it was her way to deal with having a mommy in the hospital and her way of controlling what little she could. I could not be there for her.

I could not be there for my sweet Lulu Belle as she internalized all of her fear and uncertainty, twisting it into anger with her sister's jubilation. I could not be there to help her process these feelings, to wrap my arms around her and whisper that it's normal to feel like this. She needed to hear that, and I couldn't say it.

I could not be there to answer all of Friso's questions or concerns about me or what was going to happen. I could not be there to chat with him, leaving him with a father and a sister who were bottling their feelings up; under no circumstance would they allow themselves to articulate their feelings. It's Friso's way to deliberate, to hem and haw until he finds a harmonious resolve. I left him on his own, poor bird.

I felt sentenced. I was just a bystander, observing my life from a hospital room.

Johan, with the help of Katja and Olivier, pulled Cleo's birthday party off with ease. I was deeply jealous that they were able to do all the things I couldn't, but at the same time I felt like counting my lucky stars that we had them as friends. Friends who could make a child feel super-special by doing arts and crafts or being a human jungle gym for all of her little pals. I felt grateful, mixed with an explosive cocktail of envy and bitterness.

After the party Katja and Olivier came to visit me in the hospital with their boys. It seemed like years had passed since we saw each other skiing in Hakuba. We sat in my sunroom trying like hell not to disturb the other patients on the twelfth floor with giggles that erupted more than once into full-blown fits of hysterics. It was the boys' first time in a hospital.

As they left, Boris, their oldest child shouted, "Goodbye mommy-two" and Bruno, their middle one whispered in my ear, "I love you." That warmed my heart through and through. It was enough to release my grouchy thoughts of estrangement, at least for a little while, and let me appreciate how fortunate I was to have them in my life.

# CHAPTER 6
## My side (Is All That Matters)
*Week 3: A savage cocktail, spiked with grit.*

Then the cards started to roll in. Michelle and Gordana were first. They made me cry. I was truly overwhelmed with what followed. It seemed to me that everyone who had heard the news, even those that I didn't know so well– or even at all–, were wishing me well. Just looking at those loving cards and heartfelt letters, all placed where I could see them from wherever I stood, made me strong.

Bless the homeroom moms of Cleo's class. I was astonished when a package was dropped off at the hospital containing cards from Cleo's classmates and generous gifts from their parents. Forty little souls, handwriting me cards on their little desks! I was overcome with joy. I could not manage to keep my eyes dry when reading what each and every one of those wonderful children wrote to me. Those cards got a wicked spot, above the couch, where I could fall asleep looking at them and each morning they would greet me anew! Some of them were particularly dear to me.

Like Skye's, who drew both her and me in our glasses! Our class mom, Jo, organized everything and sent them by way of a gift basket. In it, she included the most fabulous gifts a girl could ask for. A gift certificate for a pedicure, a mug, an iTunes gift certificate, chocolates—the list just kept going.

The cards and presents just kept coming in. I really don't know what I had done to deserve such royal treatment, but it truly made me happy. I plastered all the cards up on my hospital bedroom wall so I could lay in bed, surrounded by warm thoughts and well-wishes. I have kept all of them, every single one. They have helped me in my goal to become a kinder, softer version of myself.

I received flowers, chocolates, some "borrelhapjes" (a Dutch saying that means goodies served with drink) and my favorite book of all time, "Texts From Dog." I received things to renew my senses, delight my taste buds and refresh my spirit. I loved receiving flowers, cards and gifts from my "village." Some of my favorites were a fig candle to calm and a beautiful talisman for protection.

I would soon come to realize that as expats living in a foreign land, with no family surrounding us, the teachers, the friends, those intuitive, kind hearts saw what I needed. I needed more than family. This community pulled together, some of them new friends and all of them friends not longer than two-and-a-half years, no questions asked. I felt loved and needed, as if my friends and family were willing me to get better.

Gordana, my dear friend, took to making me healthy juices each day. They always came in a gorgeously wrapped bag with a handwritten card every time. Then there was my dear friend Kara, who I've known for the better part of thirty years; she was gutted by the distance that separated us. So, she started a silent campaign to let me know that she was thinking about me every single day. She knew I couldn't send text messages, so she would rattle on about her life, leaving me with the feeling of connection and closeness. She knew that I had a thing for a certain coconut lip balm. So she sent me a package to try out some other coconut lip balms! So sweet!

That's the thing about your cheerleaders: they are selfless, even when they have the most to lose. The thing that sets Kara or Gordana or Katja apart is that they never once did it for themselves. They only had my well-being at heart. The thoughtfulness, the care, comes through, even though, in Kara's case, considerable distance separates us.

At this point, I believed that I would be okay. I was completely focused on things like learning how to put my contacts in, watching my mother's endless tutorials. She was so patient with me. Watching me for thirty or forty minutes each morning while I tried to put them in and another thirty or forty minutes at the end of the day while I tried to get them out. It seemed very important for me to do this.

I was fully committed to wearing my contacts again and because they are hard contacts, getting them on and off was a delicate process. If I could not get them out, I would have to use a little plunger-like apparatus to pluck them out. If I tugged on my eye the wrong way to get them out, it would pop the contact out of its place and send it floating around in my eye. The amount of times that we had to use a flashlight to find that little thing in my eye was seriously trying. I was determined, but my mom recently told me that this scared her. If I would have placed the plunger in the wrong place, she would not have known what to do. Luckily, we didn't have that problem.

My mother was also instrumental in bringing the right clothes to me. She knew what I was looking for with just a few hand motions or grunts. Finally, I could get out of my pajamas. No one is supposed to see me in them. Only sick people stay in their pajamas for the whole day. For God's sake, I was going to therapy in them! Walking around the halls in them! I loved her so much for this. I felt like a new person, wearing my jogging leggings and sweaters once again.

I would wear the clothes and then pack them up for Johan to take them home and wash them, expecting them to be returned to me in a few days. Each night I would fold my clothes for him to bring them home. And each morning when he came back, I was surprised to see that he wasn't carrying my clean clothes. Or, even worse, when my precious clothes came back and they were destroyed! I mean what was the problem? Really, what was it? I couldn't figure it out. That really irked me that he had one job to do and, yet, it was too difficult!

The truth is that Johan carried the brunt of my stroke. He suddenly was the mom, the dad, the provider, the organizer, the man with an incredibly sick wife. The children were needy. I was needy. Doing the laundry just wasn't at the top of his list at the time. I remember asking him what the problem was with bringing my clothes back to me after they were washed. I had gall.

Johan didn't like my new enthusiasm for my contacts, either. He was being overly protective of me and, while I somehow liked this deviation from his normal, happy-go-lucky attitude, I felt that his concern was a bit too far. He made me ask my doctor on his daily visit if it was safe for me.

One day, Johan entered my room and I had a small cut on my chest, from where I couldn't say. He immediately rang the nurse, demanded that I be bandaged up, and talked to me very seriously about the fact that I was on blood thinners, so I must be careful.

From his viewpoint, although I was completely oblivious to it, he almost lost his wife. He was in shock, though at the time I had literally no clue what he was feeling. It was as if my stroke wiped me clean of any sense of compassion. He was going down a rabbit hole, not able to make any sense of it all. His spirit was drained. Johan was keeping his head above water. But barely. He couldn't handle it any more.

Unfortunately, I couldn't see this. From my blunted perspective it was all about me.

I was also becoming highly irritated by my physiotherapist. She was a bit wacky, but that's what I liked about her. Now that I was ready to bear down and I could feel it in my bones the closeness to being able to walk to physiotherapy, she was becoming lazy. While I was ready to move beyond, I had the feeling that she was holding me back.

Her routine was mechanical, like she'd done it with the patient before me and after me. I tried to communicate my plan to her. Was she even listening? Come on! I want to work! I found it extremely agitating that within a forty-minute PT session, I was spending ten of those sitting on a chair, watching her fetch things or put them back. I became exasperated with her.

More and more, I realized that there was very little that I could manage. As my mental fog dissipated, I was seeing that the whole world hadn't stopped. Just my world. I couldn't do anything about it. As reality began to sink its evil claws in, I was beginning to feel like a hanger-on in my own life.

I lacked the capacity to see anything from anyone else's point of view. I lacked the grace to be kind. Thanks to my stroke, I saw everything from one side: My side.

# CHAPTER 7
## Putting Up a Fight
*Week 4: Bulldozing the white coats.*

I was walking non-stop through the halls, thinking that everything seemed to move at a snail's pace. I could bet that the nurses were making fun of me. I didn't care. I knew what I was working towards. I was manic, fixated on achieving. At the beginning of my fourth week, my doctors signed-off on me walking, by myself, to the elevator and then down to my therapies. Imagine the time that I would save!

I was so motivated that I convinced Johan to hire another PT from outside the hospital. Joey started immediately. He would come to my room, with his bag of tricks, and we would work together. I wasn't too fond of Joey, to me he seemed like a know-it-all, but I wanted to work. After a couple of sessions, we ventured downstairs, to the courtyard of the hospital. Now there was no stopping me. I knew I could do it. I went straight up to the nurses station and requested an elevator keycard to go down to the lobby and back to the twelfth floor.

I had my first coffee in the hospital courtyard, with Gordana, that afternoon. It tasted delicious.

Little by little, reality crept in. It was like walking down a long hallway with something shining brightly through all of the doors along that very complicated and scary tunnel. Slowly, I began to realize what was really happening to me, my body and my spirit. I was more mobile and could think a bit more clearly, but I increasingly felt as if a heavy blanket were wrapped around me, like a straightjacket.

I felt something nagging at me. It was like little bombs going off inside my brain. *I could experience a re-stroke.* Then nothing. *I couldn't talk.* Then nothing. The realizations came in short waves and didn't last long. They were sporadic, and it didn't add up. I had a hard time focusing on the problem, because it was so big. Much like the medicines that were placed on my table each day, I had a hard time realizing what their purpose was and why they were so important. In stages, bit by bit, I became conscious of what happens after this. After the hospital, what was next? What was I working towards?

I was lost inside the repercussions of having a stroke. Nothing seemed logical and I was incapable of accessing my thoughts or using my intuition. Except for those random bursts of enlightenment, I was becoming unglued.

In my mind, I just had to be a good student, go to my therapies, take my pills, listen to the doctors and then all would be favorable. Then I could go home, take the children to New Zealand for their spring break, and be whole again. However, I was beginning to sense that this wasn't going to happen at all.

It was with that realization of what comes next, that I received a gift from Lorraine, the Head of School at our children's school. I was delighted that she was thinking about me. She is a legend in my mind. As I opened her card, my mouth dropped. As a good Kiwi she packaged up some magazines from her home land, because she knew that I was planning on taking our children to New Zealand for spring break. Her card reflected the fact that she knew that I had to cancel my plans, so here were some magazines to live vicariously through.

It was the first time that I realized just how bad my situation was–having to cancel my spring break plans with our children.

I didn't know what to do. I can work with a plan, any plan. I am an achiever. What happens next? Deciding to take matters into my own hands, I began secretly walking out of the hospital, walking around it's perimeter and jetting back in before anyone could see me. It seemed like a logical next step. I was afraid, but I found out much later, my brain was working off of that fear. My neurons were reorganizing themselves. My fear propelled me in the most conscious way. I was pushing myself with each secret lap around the hospital.

I kept it from Johan. When the children came for their daily visits I would covertly grab one of them and drag them with me. I felt safer with them, so I could walk longer. When I deemed that I could safely go further, I grabbed my mobile and set out to include the neighboring building in my loop. That actually panicked me. I saved that long lap for the kids' visits. In retrospect, to go outside for sneaky walks or to hire another physiotherapist or insisting to wear my contacts, is precisely what saved me.

Johan asked the doctors what they were thinking. What happens next? At my stroke's severity level and because I still needed twenty-four-hour care, the doctors were quick to suggest a rehabilitation facility. And Johan agreed.

I remember the day, like it was yesterday, when I toured Tokyo's leading rehabilitation center. Johan and I were almost giddy with anticipation. When you are in the hospital for so many weeks, the next stage, even if that stage is rehab, means that you've actually succeeded with the first part of your recovery. And that is cause for a moment, albeit brief, of cheer. That feeling of optimism was short-lived, though, as horror took its place.

It was my first morning out of the hospital; I was allowed to leave with the condition that we would have me back by lunchtime. With my mother in tow and a very kind Japanese friend, Sayuri, to translate for us, we were ready to take on this next stage of my development.

Our expectations were high. From the doctors raving about famous athletes (Japan is known for their baseball) who recuperated there, to my own image of myself getting fixed there, nothing could have prepared us for what we found. The sheer breathtaking sense of despair of this day and the panic that ensued, will haunt my memories for a long time to come.

The patients were all seemingly locked in a jail, for a crime that I can only assume they did not commit. None of them looked in any way happy; in fact they were like zombies. I found it difficult to envision myself living side by side with these shadows.

I had envisioned something totally different. Not that there's anything wrong with it, because let's face it, we are all going to be old one day, but in my mind I kind of pictured young ball players instead of people with an average age of ninety-four. It was hard to see. There was no life, no joy. Just listless souls, succumbing to their environment.

Then we came around to the part of the tour which I was actually looking forward to, the part where all the baseball players would fight to recover and I myself was going to make leaps and bounds on my own recovery: the sports complex. When the guide told me that I could use the gym for two forty-minute sessions per day and only then under close supervision of my trainer, I wanted to scream! What? How the hell would this benefit me! I was sick with the thought! I had heard that the first three months were crucial to my recovery and that I had to get the most out of it. I didn't see how this limited access would allow me to do that. I felt besieged.

Next we talked about what my daily life would look like. I would have to undergo a medical exam to see if I could shower alone, or if I would need an aide to help. As I was already showering alone, I found this completely frustrating. I couldn't advocate for myself because my aphasia wouldn't allow it and, even if I could talk, the language barrier was standing between us. I wanted to scream. Looking back, I shudder to think that I dared to shower alone. It scares the shit out of me. I was irrational and oblivious due to my brain damage and the risks didn't even dawn on me. To this day, I still have problems standing in the shower and utilize one of those rubber bath mats (that old people use) to stabilize myself. Looking back, I secretly agree with the rehab center's caution. But at the time, I didn't want to hear it.

I would have to eat every meal in the cafeteria, side by side with the other patients. Think about it; who would I speak to? Who would speak to me? I would have to have permission and a special pass to go outside. Not getting a breath of fresh air, at one's will, seemed like a slow form of torture for me. I was trembling.

I pictured myself stuck, like a rat in its cage. I wanted to thrash someone. I was overwhelmed with the feeling of defeat. My fists were clenched and ready to pummel with rage. Some of these things I could possibly live with on their own, maybe even two or three, but the combination of all of them, pressing me down, making me feel like an infant, was just too much. I had to get out of there.

After the tour and after our talk about my daily life, we talked about the details of my stay. I would stay there for three months. It was unclear if I could continue with my speech therapist, Seth, virtually. Although, as we pointed out, it was impossible for me to work with the Japanese therapists, who only spoke in Japanese. What the heck? What didn't they understand?

The biggest assault came when I was told that there was no private room with a bathroom attached. Even if I were allowed to shower on my own, without an aide, there would be no private place to do so. I would be placed in a shared room and have to shower communally. I wanted to die, or at the very least, run away.

I left with a feeling of doom and aggression. Helplessness rose from my stomach and stuck in my throat. You see, someone might walk the same walk that I did that day. And that someone might have a very different reaction to it. However, I was suffering the massive effects of my stroke. My injured brain just saw red.

If my stroke had happened somewhere that was not so foreign, so strange to me, if it had been familiar in any way, I might have accepted my fate and gracefully gone to the rehabilitation facility. But I couldn't wrap my head around the fact that I couldn't go outside without permission, that I would be made to eat in the cafeteria or deal with those other convalescents, those passive souls, who were simply obeying. I could not shower in a group. I hadn't done that since high school gym class and even then I felt disgust. It's different in Japan. Communal bathing is a celebrated part of their culture and, in general, there is peace in conformity. I could not accept many aspects of this place because, culturally, it was too far from my habits.

In short, the center repulsed me.

The rest of that day became one which I cannot, and should not, forget. I took my anger, my rage, and turned my destructive behavior on anyone that was in my way. I fought with my mother, Sayuri, my best friend, and my husband, as well as any doctors or nurses who dared to get in my way. I was unstoppable, on a path leading to my own destruction. I was terrible. My anger was visible despite my messed-up communication style. I was silently cursing them in my head and wishing that they would all go away.

On the taxi ride back to the hospital, my mother, the kindest soul I've ever met, annoyed the shit out of me. I remember her gabbing about having a glass or two of wine and discussing with Johan where to have it. I just wanted her to shut up. Wasn't she in the same meeting that I was in? Her diminutive problems definitely seemed to pale in comparison to my cruel obstacles.

Of course, her situation was a little bit more complicated than that. She was witnessing her forty-six year old daughter struggling with simple tasks like brushing her teeth and balancing. I later learned that she spent many nights, during the weeks she spent taking care of me, crying. My mother was and is a saint. She never, ever let me see her sweat. She didn't miss a single PT or OT session and she was present for many of my speech therapy calls also.

Of course she was entirely entitled to a glass, or even bottle, of wine. I was just being a bitch. In my condition, things were either black or white and I was either happy or sad. My emotions were not within my control. I know that now, and in fact I am extremely embarrassed by this. But at the time, it seemed that my mother was completely selfish. If I'm honest, gaining control of my emotions has been much more taxing than teaching my right hand to grasp a chopstick and feed myself. I know that if the food lands on my lap, I didn't do it correctly. But shouting at my children or making my husband feel like shit or the feeling of disdain for my mother has a lasting effect. One that I wish I hadn't experienced.

On the one hand, I just wanted to kick myself that I'd believed in the hype of the Japanese rehab center. I mean, how stupid could I be? Everyone knows that Japan has a graying population, and everyone knows that old people generally get strokes. What was I thinking–that handsome baseball players would meet me as we recovered together, and shower me with season tickets in the owner's box? How foolish.

I got back from the center just in time for lunch, which was disgusting. It didn't bother me so much, but I would like a decent meal from time to time. And on this infuriating day, it seemed like an extra insult.

I was just about to take a nap before I went on with Seth, when Katja arrived with lunch for me. It was one of my favorites and I began to loosen up from my morning. Good food has that effect on me. As we chatted about the rehabilitation center, with my half-language, half-gesture and a good friend to interpret it all, I declared that if that was the Japanese level of rehabilitation care, then I would happily live like this, like a shadow of myself. I was so dispirited and appalled by our visit that I felt no option. I couldn't go there. The thought crippled me. I told her that I would rather not get better and just learn to live my life like a victim.

She was stunned.

She considered this, asking me questions about the center. She was probing deeply. Looking back, I should have stopped her, eaten the lunch that I so desperately wanted to eat, and that she'd lovingly bought for me to enjoy, and gotten some rest. But she was probing too deeply. I started to fume. My emotions were in a state of combat. I was triggered by the failure of my first morning out of the hospital and pure fatigue. In the end, I said something that I shouldn't have. I don't even remember what. It was nasty, borderline vicious, and, above all, hurtful.

If the shoe were on the other foot I don't know what I would have done. Katja told me that I needed some rest. *Rest? What?* She then picked up her racket and left to go get Squidgy some medicine from our apartment because she was running a fever.

The Squidge had contracted smacked-face-syndrome, a relatively harmless infection that gets its name from the bright, rosy cheeks it causes. Although I could not do much about it, it struck me that I wasn't there to cuddle her, to take her temperature or to make sure that she was drinking enough. In my heart I knew that it wasn't anything that Katja and Johan couldn't handle, and in some cases probably better than me.

My damaged brain couldn't shake the feeling that I was somehow being replaced. Through no fault of my own, and even despite me, my children were being taken care of by someone other than their mother.

Of course, that's poppycock. They would have loved me to be there, packing their lunches and tucking them in, but I was damn lucky that Katja and Johan could step in. The worst part about living abroad is that it is far away from family. The funny thing is though, Katja and her family joined ours the minute I suffered my stroke.

Be that as it may, sometimes your family is just there to annoy the shit out of you, or so I thought in that instance.

I had had enough of Katja, with her smart mouth, telling me that I needed some rest. How dare she play tennis all morning and then pick up lunch for her sick friend on her way to the hospital? I never ate that lunch. I still remember the empty feeling of triumph as I tipped it into the bin when she left. I was seething and thought that this would teach her! Telling me that I needed to rest! I'll show her.

As I walked to the kitchen, to dispose of the food my friend had spent time and money on, something was nagging at me. It was a complicated, mixed-up feeling. Was it shame? Guilt? Whatever it was, it was foreign to me and my injured brain. All I felt as I was tipping the food into the bin was self-righteous satisfaction. And then massive sadness.

As I lay down to take a nap before my speech therapy session, my mind could not switch off. It obsessed over everything. The rehab. My mother. Katja. My poor baby, Cleo. What was the name of the medicine that I give to the kids when they have a temperature? It starts with an A, doesn't it? Oh! I know! It's Algifor. I have to call my mother straight away!

I cannot even begin to recap the conversation that followed. In my mind it went like this, but of course I couldn't speak, so it couldn't have possibly gone like this:

"Hi mom, I know the medicine. It's called…"

And just like that, my mind went blank. Even over the phone wire, I could tell that I was stressing my mother. I didn't care. My daughter's life was at stake!

"Put Katja on the phone," I demanded.

Katja came on the line.

"Katja, go into my bathroom closet and read to me all of the medicines on the upper shelf," I huffed.

I wouldn't describe Katja as a patient woman, but her restraint in not telling me to go to hell that day was testament to the powers of our friendship. She began listing, one by one, all of them.

I was getting frustrated. I couldn't think of the specific medicine! I couldn't imagine that Cleo would be fine, if Katja didn't know which medicine I would have given her. Of course she was fine because she was a healthy little girl who had a minor fever. Yet for me, in that moment, Katja represented all that I was not. She was strong, while I was feeble. She was mobile, while I couldn't leave the hospital ward. She had access.

So, I let her have it. All of it. Without holding back. I certainly was not entitled to shout at my friend, my lifeline to the outside world. I hung up the phone feeling supremely justified with my appalling behavior.

I saw everything blocking me from my recuperation and didn't yet see the opportunity. So I gave in to my stroke that day. I moved aside and let the demons take over. There were so many of them and they were crashing down, so I decided to let them win. Even in my reduced state, I knew that there had to be another option for me.

My role as mother and as a woman was reduced to that of hanger-on. I was now fully in the spectator's chair. I was simultaneously feeling lost, like they were a part of a club and no one invited me in, and ashamed for feeling this way.

The week ended with the school's Spring Concert, starring every student in the school, and my first daily release from the hospital. I was going to go home for the first time in a month, if only for the day! I found it electrifying and I couldn't stop shaking with excitement while waiting for my family to come pick me up. I was waiting, coat in hand, just like an over-enthusiastic child, for what seemed like hours in my sunroom.

The plan was they would pick me up on their way from the Spring Concert and we would walk to our place with

Katja's tribe. Although I would have given my eye teeth to watch my three perform, I knew I wasn't ready for that. The noises would be unbearable and the commotion, mixed with my uncertainty, would be cruel to put me through. As it was, Johan was not prepared for the barrage of sympathetic, albeit unwanted intrusions that he faced on this day. It was his first time in public since my stroke.

Each time the elevator would ding, I would look up expectantly until I saw my four in all of their vigor. I thought my heart would pound right out of my skin. It was really happening! I was theirs until nine o'clock that night. We walked the short distance home, their excited voices recapping what I'd missed. I was content.

Arriving at our home might have been intimidating; the last time I was there the paramedics had to shuffle me out. However, the house was filled with love and family. There wasn't anything scary about it. We ate dinner, the others drank champagne on my behalf; but, by seven o'clock, it was too much. The loudness, the excitement, and the joy of being home were making me feel insecure. I was tired from the emotion and from the week. I had to ask Johan if I could leave early. He walked me back to my hospital room at seven-fifteen.

They had let me into their club and, sadly, I could not keep up.

# CHAPTER 8
## A Plan and a Fight
*Weeks 5 - 6: Crafted carefully through the eyes and the mind of a survivor.*

Now the hard part began...

By the fifth week in the hospital, I began to get really impatient. I'd had it with the disgusting food. I was losing weight.

Katja never once, over the course of six weeks, missed a day visiting me in the hospital. Bringing me my daily coffee and food when she realized that I was losing weight. She was there for every meeting with the doctors and every interview with therapists. She was there, with her sarcastic humor, making me laugh despite my shitty luck. She was there to claw onto, to make me believe that I could get better. And all the while, she was taking care of her husband and her own three children.

Still, I was ready to make the next move.

So I had to get my team on board. There were a few things I knew for sure. I wanted to have my rehabilitation my way. No cookie-cutter approach. I knew that it had to be now. I was too aware that every moment spent thinking about the work that lay ahead of me, and not doing the work, was a moment wasted.

It was anything but easy. At this time of my life, my head was still quite foggy. I had trouble speaking and thinking. In fact my speech was all jumbled up in a mismatched salad of nonsense. It took me forever to think of the next word that I was going to say and then I forgot what I had said just before. It was frustrating to live in a state of limbo, having lucid thoughts flicker briefly across my consciousness before they disappeared. Even so, I began to question my doctors about my recovery.

Culturally, in Japan, there is no place for those who question people of authority. My doctors had proposed the thing that they propose to all people who have a stroke: the rehabilitation center. And I dared to question that approach. Although they perhaps would have liked to help me out, they seemed incapable, like my reasonable questions suddenly hit deaf ears.

It's like a wall was built around their version of the truth. Everything inside that wall works like a dream. You don't ask questions. You simply accept their version of the truth, as your truth. You have a stroke and then you go to the first rehab center which they politely order you to, posed in the form of an invitation that you should not turn down. If you dare to ask for another rehab center, to see a second one as I did, you are a source of embarrassment to the doctors. They have lost their control of the situation and lost face to the first rehab facility. Their pride was smashed.

The doctors, perhaps, didn't see me coming. I was a foreigner. I was young. And I was taught from early on that if you don't like the situation, then you should change it. I would like to think that they wanted to help me, but instead, I appeared to be alienating them. I was devastated by the notion that I had asked too many questions about my recovery, basically causing them to throw their hands up in the air out of bewilderment. It felt as if they just wanted nothing to do with me. I had a stroke. I was in a foreign land. No one understood me. It felt like I was alone, situated in a big black hole of dark confusion.

At that point I was five weeks post stroke. My head was not clear; in fact I couldn't remember my address or the names of my children. I referred to myself as he and my husband as I. I saw the problem at hand, and even through my fuzziness, I realized that none of my doctors knew me or could find a solution that worked for me. They just didn't know how it made me feel to be lost, abandoned in a city that wasn't home to me. The feeling of desolation crept over me and sat there, just sat there begging me to not let it overtake me.

This was an extremely grim and bleak time for me. A time of extreme adversity. It was a moment in which I saw nothing but obstacles facing me, obstacles that I couldn't do anything about.

It was a moment when I took stock of my situation and precisely the moment when I, being a strong willed, fire-eater of a girl, took matters into my own hands. This time was no different. The stroke didn't take that drive away from me. My scrappiness, my determination and, above all, my will.

You see, that big bonfire of tenacity surfaced in the most serendipitous way. It was like something awoke in my soul, urging me to recognize the power I had. Power over myself and the ability to impact everything that happens to me. It was like coming out of a deep, dark, cozy slumber. This urge, the scent, awakens your basic instincts. My basic instincts were screaming, "Wake up! Smell the coffee! And get on with it!".

This was a defining moment of my stroke and my life.

I was many things to many different people before my stroke. I was a wife who gave up her business and moved the whole family to Tokyo in support of her husband. I was a mother who gave it my all, from organizing school charity events, to sitting on the bleachers watching yet another football game to my newly found habit of cooking up a storm each night.

After my stroke, I was simply a survivor.

Of all the things that my stroke took away from me–my stories, my voice and a certain wind from my sails–it was here, at this moment, that I realized my fire. I was a creator.

A cunning plan started brewing in my head. If I didn't go to rehab, could I make rehab come to me? The thought left me in a euphoric state. I couldn't shake the feeling that this was exactly what I needed. I became obsessed with my plans for myself. I confided my secret intentions to Seth, who responded in a very matter of fact manner. He ran through the pros and cons, which only further fueled my desire to blaze my own trail to recovery.

I would wake up every morning thinking about recovering from home and go to sleep dreaming about it. I had to find a way to harness my forces and forge ahead. Could I get my team on board? Would I be safe? Could I build an effective program of therapies? How could a woman without her voice accomplish this? As I saw it, from my muddy, obscured view, it looked like a tangled-up web. Johan would be the key to unlock this opportunity for me.

Unfortunately, things were getting progressively worse between Johan and I. We were bickering nonstop. I felt disconnected from him. I needed him to stay with me, to lie with me and to shut the world out with me. Me. Me. Me. Me. I couldn't sympathize with him and dismissed all of the other constraints on his time. I was frustrated by my chaotic, blurred language and my scrambled cognitive reasoning skills. I was simultaneously reaching for him and, when I didn't get the response that I needed, pushing him away with my criticisms. I couldn't tell him that he was hurting me.

On the other side of the spectrum, Johan seemed to just shut his ears and vomit out all the things that were pressing down on him. If I only had a dime for the times that I had to hear about how much he had on his plate, I thought I'd be a rich girl. It seemed that it was me against him. And around we went. Me, engulfed with the paralyzing aftermath of my stroke, and Johan, overburdened and overwhelmed with it all. We couldn't break the circle. He felt criticized and overwrought with the situation, and I felt overlooked, ignored and small. I felt like he was replacing me.

It was so unfair. Had we been in an English-speaking country, perhaps a counselor could have intervened. I just wanted him to take me in his arms and protect me, but all he could see, and frankly all I showed him, was an aggressive, sick wife.

He went out for drinks three times that week, including one time where he was meeting a colleague for work and wanted to meet his friends afterwards. In talking about it beforehand, I tried to explain my insecurities to him. I was anxious for the children and how they would handle being left with the babysitter while their mother was stuck in a hospital and their father out in a bar. I understood that his job expected this from him, although I was sure that in this situation he could be excused, but I couldn't wrap my head around why he seemed to need it. I truly felt that he should remain available for our children. I would have been. Honestly, it felt wrong to me, like escapism.

Sadly, he didn't feel the same. We had words which ended in him promising not to go, presumably just to get me off his back. The shame of it is, he did go. I was hurt beyond belief; at that point, the whole world seemed unfair. My heart was cracked open and bleeding. I resigned myself to the fact that this concrete world was my life now, without escape. My husband was disengaging.

A series of questions come to mind that I still have trouble answering. How do you begin to repair the damages? Those which were there before? Those which were broken in the first place? Were we broken? It certainly felt this way then. Surviving a stroke clouds your peripheral view. Unrelenting absoluteness was all I could feel. As mad as I was at Johan for breaking my trust, I simply filed it in the deepest folds of my mind and trusted that we would find our way.

At the forefront of my mind was the fact that I wanted the best for my therapy and also myself. To me, the most important thing about my recovery was that I could smile at the beginning and end of each day. The days would be long and hard, but I expected this. I craved this chance to learn, to take action. Thus, it had to be a place where I felt happy. I needed that space.

There were a few aspects which were of utmost importance to me, in fact I couldn't get them out of my head. It was like being all alone with my thoughts, circulating like a wild kaleidoscope of butterflies, just waiting for me to tame them and make them mine. For starters, I was results-driven. My leg *would* run again, my hand *would* write again and my voice *would* carry for many years to come. The me I was visualizing was concrete, brute, and almost animalistic.

As this new Stacie was starting to crystallize from within, I hit many walls. I was no longer mute. In fact by now I could make my opinions known to most. (The poor nurses could attest to this.) That was not the problem. The problem was trying to make the pieces of the puzzle fit together and controlling all of the crazy, foreign influences surrounding me.

My inability, here in this moment, to formulate complete, actionable thoughts was something that I was going to vanquish come hell or high water. I had to focus on this goal in order to make well thought-through, legible, and convincing arguments for myself.

So I got cracking on the one thing that I was able to control: articulating what my recovery would look like. I began on my journey slowly, deliberately formulating a plan from my hospital bedside. I wrote my goals for my therapies. Line by line I wrote, for more than two hours each day, until the words formed magic in front of my eyes.

I outlined what I needed from my therapists and what they should know about me. I started with each goal I could think of, from all areas of my life, ranging from the physical (such as tennis - I just wanted the chance to beat Katja!) to the cognitive (I wanted to write a book!) to the emotional (how would I calm down when the demons came hollering?) and everything in between.

From there, I delineated what it would take to meet each goal that I set for myself. For instance, beating Katja at tennis was just a dream that I conjured up, a spark to light the fire of my competitiveness, to get me going in the right direction.

To actually meet this goal, I had to think about every step. This was the tough part because it required me to think cognitively about what tennis is and how to be back on my game. It was the first time that I took an active role in deciding what my recovery would look like. I didn't like the rehab facilities; in fact they made me feel awful. But I was not going to go down without a fight. If I was put there, it would not be because I acquiesced easily.

So I wrote on. I had to list my questions to ask my doctors and therapists. Could I safely play tennis? What could I do to improve my power and range? How could the room stop spinning so I could actually hit the ball?

Once I was done with that list I made another one of skills, which I definitely took for granted pre-stroke. I had to improve my gait, my grip strength, speed, agility, power and range of motion for my hands and for my legs, and improve my endurance so I could play for fifteen minutes, thirty minutes, forty-five minutes, one hour! Until I had the endurance to beat Katja at the game we both love so much!

I began with a blank sheet and watched as my wishes transformed into a plan. For someone suffering from brain damage, suffering from non-fluent aphasia and agraphia, it was a hell of a lot of work. Working intensely with Seth, I set out to change the course of my recovery. I very meticulously, over the course of weeks, made a plan for myself. It wasn't easy. In fact, when I reflect upon it now, I am filled with amazement and wonderment. I worked two hours per day, seven days a week, for one month. Or, sixty hours. When I completed them, I was proud. My goals would carry me a long way, giving me motivation, giving me the desire to do better, quicker.

It was then that I made the hard choice. To fight. To find new ways to carve out the new me. I learned that I had to be my own biggest advocate. No one could or would do it for me in a way that was acceptable. I wasn't doing it for my children or my husband. I was going to get better for me, and I was preparing myself for the long run.

My goals – taken directly from my computer:
(written over painstakingly long sessions with Seth)
PHOTOGRAPHY
1) Get my hands attuned to the function of working
    my camera, so that I don't miss a shot because I
    wasn't ready
    a) Find my base line
    b) Work up to 5 seconds
2) Get my feet tuned-up to go 5-10 km for a photo
    walk
    a) Develop the balance so I feel like I can
        trust myself again
    b) Develop the faith in myself, that my body,
        my mind and the world are coming
        together for the moment
3) Dream time -

WRITING
1) Continue to write my blog, as a bread-crumb-path
    from where my journey started to where it's going
    to next
    a) I can quickly and effortlessly write down
        my work
    b) Get my hands attuned to the function of
        writing
    c) Concentrate on what I want to say, writing
        correctly what I want to say and getting the
        word order correct
    d) Get my endurance up to snuff - a solid two
        hours of meaningful text
    e) Develop my own clear voice
        i) Read my voice
How my fave author express his/her self
2) Write my book

   a) Writing 20 blog posts in my "own voice"
   b) Daily journaling of my ideas
      i) Take a moment to review my memories of my days
   c) The IDEA!!
      i) At the beginning of every month I write down where I am at with the idea
   d) Litmus test the idea ("sanity check")
   e) Write
      i) 20 page per day

3) Texting
   a) Take a minute to make sure that each stroke is the correct one

4) Placeholder for "fate"

## PHYSICAL ACTIVITY

1) Play tennis - go for a lesson, or play set with Katja
   a) At the next MRI, send a question list to the doctor ahead of time, including tennis
      i) Can I run safely
      ii) Can ride my bike
      iii) Can I safely be alone
      iv) Medicine for constipated
      v) Optical consultation
      vi) Wine?
      vii) Sex?
      viii) What are chances re-stroke
      ix) When my next MRI
      x) Is it possible to have the mid June
   b) Improve my gait
      i) PT _ placeholder
   c) Improve speed, agility, power and range of motion for my hands and for my legs

          i)      Ask my OT
          ii)     Ask my PT

  d)  Improve my endurance
          i)      Rallying for 15 minutes
          ii)     Playing 15 minutes
          iii)    Playing 30 minutes
          iv)    Playing 45 minutes
          v)     Playing 1 HOUR

  e)  Beat Katja!

2)  Run - 5 kms / 3 days of the week
  a)  I need to work on my balance
          i)      Balance exercises
          ii)
  b)  I need to work all 5 senses
  c)  I need to improve my speed
  d)  Improve my endurance

## BE KIND TO MYSELF

1)  Tell yourself what you would say to others in your situation
  a)  Interrupt my thoughts
          i)      Create awareness that I am hell-bent on something
          ii)     Create a positive switch-over statement
  b)  Tell myself it's ok
          i)      Then decide *what's it going to be?*
          ii)     Accept your decision

2)  Xxx

## PERSONAL GOALS

1)  Become a softer version of myself
  a)  Identify that "20%" (that I don't want to be / think / say)

    b) Create a positive switch-over statement
       i) I own this imperfection and I love myself with it.
    c) Trust the process
    d) Share my imperfections with pride, as the whole me

2) Develop a mantra
    a) Identify my mantra
    b) Set my timer to go off 30-45 times per day
    c) Identify the times when my mantra goes automatically
    d) Identify the times when my mantra needs to go automatically
    e) Consistently use my mantra in 80% of situations that cause me stress

3) Meditation
    a) Find a time to meditate
    b) Find a track that works
    c) Enjoy the time to be by myself

*If you want to make goals for yourself in order to find your passion, visit my website www.staciebroek.com. Click "Free Tools" in the main menu.*

I was so engrossed in making a clear-cut plan for myself, I didn't realize that I was alienating my doctors to the point where they were fed up with me, although this got them on-board with my plan. I had no idea why I had somehow managed to convince them to let me convalesce at home. Were they just as confused as I? I found that funny and more than a little distressing. One minute they were strong-arming me to choose the date in which I would leave for the rehabilitation center and the next they were sure that I didn't need a rehabilitation center. In fact, I still remember the day they were making their rounds and they announced, quite joyfully, that I could go home. When did I want to be discharged? What?? I was baffled.

It's curious how something can get that lost in translation. I remember people, doctors, nurses and even my physiotherapist asking me if I was going to stay or if I was going to go. I genuinely had no idea what they were talking about. It was as if they had held a secret meeting to decide my fate without me.

I will never quite understand what happened to change their minds. Had I asked too many questions? Had I not been a good patient? It was no use to inquire about this. Between my tangled language and their English, the answer seemed elusive.

I remember feeling completely stressed about this. I shuddered to think of what Johan would say. How would he respond to the fact that I had apparently convinced my doctors that I should go home?

On one hand, I had won! On the other hand, I seriously felt scared of what that meant. To be away from my doctors was alarming; my whole world had revolved around them for the past six weeks. I was stuck in the middle of wanting to go home so badly, but knowing that the hospital was where I felt safest. The possibility of re-stroke haunted me. I was stricken with fear. I didn't know anything about strokes before, and now my life was centered around the thoughts and images of me dying in front of my children.

Likewise, from the moment I saw the first rehabilitation center, I was hell-bent on going home to recover. In fact, the very thought of being put in such a place could bring me to tears. I couldn't see myself getting well there, but I had to dig deeper into the possibilities. Was it even feasible to recover at home? Was it possible to find enough therapists to fit all of my needs and if so, could I manage that? And then, what about my safety? It was almost impossible, too big, to consider by myself and my damaged brain. Every noise, even every thought that drifted through my head, clouded my sensibilities.

Nonetheless, I was driven to make it work. Even though I was scared, my drive to succeed superseded all else. By that time, we had found two speech therapists and a handful of physical therapists, but no occupational therapists. Maybe that would have dampened the spirits of some, but I continued to steamroll my way forward.

I knew on some level that piecing together a schedule would be very useful to convince Johan, so with Seth's help, I began working on it. That was a bit different from the other writing that I had accomplished thus far, because it involved skills that I had lost. For instance, making a table, counting, and thinking about the overall structure of a day. So, before I left the hospital, I created a daily schedule and followed it to a T, until it was obsolete. And then, I created a new one. And followed that one.

Now, it was only down to Johan. If I couldn't convince him, I would bulldoze him.

My daily schedule: (as taken straight from my writings with Seth...can you spot the misspelled word?)

|  | Schedule (weekday) | Schedule (weekend) |
|---|---|---|
| 6.45 | Wake up |  |
| 6.45 - 7.00 | Stretch | Stretch |
| 7.00 - 7.45 | Get ready |  |

| | | |
|---|---|---|
| 7.45 - 8.00 | Eat breakfast | |
| 8.00 - 8.10 | Brush my teeth - do my mouth exercise | Brush my teeth - do my mouth exercise |
| 8.10 - 8.30 | Taxi to physio | |
| 8.30 - 9.30 | Physio | |
| 9.30 - 10.30 | Walk back + Coffee | Physio |
| I want to use ½ hour increments | Cooking, listening to music, practice my exercised, napping, photography, walking, | |
| | Mediate (requirement) | |
| | Writing (requirement) | |
| 12.45 - 13.45 | Lunchtime | |
| 14.00 - 15.00 | Seth | Seth |

| 15.15 - 16.00 | OT | |
| 16.00 - 17.00 | Speech | |
| 17.00 - 18.45 | Time with the children | Time with children |
| 18:45 - 19.00 | Buffer | |
| 19.00 - 20.00 | Seth | Seth |
| 20.00 - 20.15 | Stretch | Stretch |
| 20.15 - 21.00 | Johan | |
| 21.00 - 21.15 | Brush my teeth - do my mouth exercise | Brush my teeth - do my mouth exercise |
| 21.15 - 21.30 | Mediate | |

*If you want to download a recovery journal based on this one, you can find it on my website: www.staciebroek.com. Click "Free Tools" in the main menu.*

Armed with my goals, my schedule and taking advice from my newfound friend, Seth, I was ready to lay the groundwork for Johan.

You see, I had to play out every scenario in my head, from finding the right therapists to setting their schedules, from the roles we would play in the family to how logistically it would work– not to mention the basics of coercing Johan to go along with my cunning plan at all!

I will always remember the day that I finally convinced Johan to let me recover from home. We were on our way back from seeing the second rehab facility. This facility was slightly different from the first, but I felt just as black, as hopeless, from it. We met with the head of the facility and he, in perfect English, explained that it would take me a minimum of six and possibly up to twelve weeks to recover. I just felt deflated by the thought of spending any time in this pit.

For instance, there was a rooftop garden that you were only allowed to visit when you had a trainer with you. Which was thirty minutes per day. Children were not allowed to visit you. You could not go outside without a special permit. Of course we were in Japan and the speech therapy was done in Japanese, but they had to consider whether or not to allow me to bring in my own virtual speech therapist. This was par for the Japanese-course. Nothing outside their norm could be considered without a huge hullabaloo.

The fact remained that I would have been willing to go to a rehab facility if I'd thought it would help me recover. I just did not see how not seeing my children (those cute faces that somehow prodded me to do the work), not being allowed to have a breath of fresh air, and having access to trainers less than two hours per day would help. To top it all off, my stroke's main effect was aphasia. I was in desperate need of speech and language therapy, and not in Japanese.

We were sitting in the taxi returning to the hospital and I turned to Johan. He just knew. He knew that I was bound and determined to recover from home. And that I might be right.

As I still needed twenty-four-hour care, Johan wanted to hire a nurse. This made me angry and the feeling of helplessness was overwhelming. I was sure I didn't need a nurse! Why was that necessary? However, as I sat through the one and only interview that the hospital could arrange, I felt my anger slowly dissipating. Suga was warm, gentle, and I could tell immediately that she cared. We were lucky, in the end. Not only that the hospital had arranged the only English-speaking nurse that was available, but to have access to an accomplished and interesting nurse like Suga made it seem like something I could handle, instead of an imposition that I couldn't tolerate.

I was going home next week. To my family. To my life. The thought of reconnecting with my children made my heart sing. I had planned every facet in detail from my schedule to how I would get enough rest. How was I going to get through the final week in the hospital? Every minute seemed like an eternity.

What made it infinitely more painful was that, during my last week in the hospital, the kids were on Spring Break. We were all supposed to go to New Zealand, the four of us. I knew that, due to my stroke, it was not possible to travel. Still, it was so difficult for me not to be with them then. My heart was breaking.

To try to make the week fun for the kids, Johan made a plan with Katja that she would take all six children to a funpark. I was so nervous. The thing is, I was a nervous mother even before the stroke. The stroke just added another level to my anxiety. I didn't sleep most of the night before and I was in a bad mood during the day of the trip.

However, I thought I played it cool—no text messages, no phone calls.

Still, sitting there waiting for any sign of life was unbearable. After my evening speech therapy session I couldn't stand it any longer. I was sleepy and I wanted to speak to the children before I went to bed. I texted Katja. When the return SMS came, explaining that they were just on their way back, I was shocked. I was borderline irate. It was very late to have the children on a train, coming back into Tokyo!

When I tried to explain my feelings to Johan, I felt that the spring had sprung. He didn't want to hear it. He just kept telling me that he was their father and he's allowed to make plans for them. I wanted to say that yes, of course you are allowed but, please include me in those plans. I wanted to make those decisions *with* him.

I was tired after six weeks of being in that prison, having no control over my body, my children, and my thoughts. To some extent, it felt like I was obsolete, like no one could see me. The overwhelming thoughts of despair hit me like a ton of bricks.

But I didn't have a say.

I remember sitting on my bed in a numb state with my legs under the covers, feeling sorry for myself. All of a sudden, I felt as if someone had stabbed me in the foot. It was the side affected by the stroke, where I'd lost all sensation, and the sensation was shocking. I screamed out loud. With caution I pulled back the covers, expecting a large insect to have bitten me. What I actually found was a hangnail on my big toe—and I could feel it! I wanted to shout from the rafters with joy! I wanted to call Johan immediately and boast about the best news of the week, that I had experienced sensation on my affected foot! I felt so much joy in that moment. As I reached for my mobile,

# (al)ONE

I remembered the argument we'd just had, and I realized when you've alienated the person you want to tell the most, you are a bit stuck.

# CHAPTER 9
## The Sweetest Reward of All
*Weeks 7 - 8: Pain, uncertainty and exhaustion are first-class prizes.*

My hard work had paid off! I was finally going home.

In preparation, Johan ordered a boatload of treats for my doctors and nurses and I wrapped them with Lulu's help. I think that in Western countries, this would have been considered normal. However, you could have heard a pin drop when I and my family delivered them at the nurses' station. I don't know if it was because they were shocked or thought that I was having another stroke, but there was a lot of looking at their shoes and bowing. My final faux pas!

Coming home after six weeks was exhilarating and more than a little nerve-wracking. I came home to a wounded relationship with my husband, which made me mad. He felt it. I felt it. We didn't know how to deal with it, so we didn't. It made me angry to come home to a house with no flowers. Johan had gone out for drinks straight from work the previous evening, not affording him the opportunity to buy them for my homecoming. I thought that that was shitty of him.

He made our older two stay home to make a banner for me, while he went to fetch me from the hospital. I was so annoyed. They belonged with me on such a momentous occasion! For them it was also symbolic and I felt that we needed this for closure. I wanted to walk out of that concrete jungle flanked by my whole family. Why couldn't the banner have been made yesterday? Until this day, I remember the hurt.

The truth is somewhere caught in between. What matters is that all Johan heard was me berating him and all I could feel was left out. We were spiraling down a wicked path of destruction.

Our three children and my husband were in for a real treat. What they knew about taking care of a stroke survivor could easily fit in their collective thumbnails. I found it hard to measure up to their desires, wants and wishes. They were so starved for their mother's attention, they found it difficult to understand that I just was not the person who left them six weeks ago.

They did their best, although I didn't make it easy on them. Johan forewarned the children that, in order for me to get well, I would have to focus on myself. He explained to them that what I needed was space to do my therapies, a place to rest after the long days and patience. The doctors and my therapists didn't help them understand. Had we been home, in Switzerland or any other place that seemed less foreign, I suppose that a therapist would have bridged their expectations. We were in uncharted territory, just like a ship lost at sea. We were trying like mad to make it work, because the thought of me recuperating anywhere else but at home seemed wrong for all of us.

Because of the true risk of re-stroke, I had enlisted the help of my mother to perform research on the best app or device that could save my life if necessary. I found it tremendously challenging to relinquish that task for two reasons. My mother lives in the United States, making it difficult for her to know what services were available in Japan, and I couldn't perform the simplest research for her. She eventually decided that my best bet was an Apple Watch.

I recall the fear of going to the Apple Store. It was my first outing in over six weeks, not counting the disastrous trips to the rehab centers. In an effort to beat the crowds, we arrived early just as it was opening. We were helped straight away by a kind twenty-something who didn't make me feel strange because I couldn't speak when he spoke to me, and swiftly moved us downstairs where the crowd was less dense and I could sit.

The anxiety when I noticed another mom from school was palpable. Should I talk to her? Was it rude if I didn't? Did she know about me? These questions were running through my mind, making me crazy with worry. They are also questions which wouldn't have sprung to my mind just six weeks before. It was like watching a pot of water as it's ready to reach the boiling point. At some point it's going to bubble and, if you're not careful, you're left with a mess.

I did manage to talk to that mom, with Johan's support. She was kind, asked immediately after my health, and commiserated with all that I was going through. As a physiotherapist, she'd seen many stroke survivors, so my condition was less incomprehensible to her.

I cannot explain the utter bewilderment, the confusion, and the resulting unease that the Apple Watch brought about. It was like having a naughty alien on my wrist. I could not make it behave, and even worse, it kept beeping at me. The children were ready and willing to help. Of course they were–it was a brand new Apple product. And, of course I was insistent on figuring it out by myself. That didn't stop me from swearing at the damn thing.

Johan continued his new routine of getting the children off to school each morning while I got ready for my first therapy session. He even fed me breakfast! That was something that I wouldn't have imagined before my stroke. Because rest was so important to me and my healing brain, Lulu gave up her bedroom for me, while she slept on a futon in Friso's room. Sleeping was tough for us all. I am not sure who benefited the most when Squidge took my spot sleeping next to Johan.

All the way through this ordeal, they have been rock stars, trying to understand me and my limitations from the get-go. Friso even developed this uncanny ability to understand me and my crazy-mixed-up language skills, even when I couldn't get the words out. For my children, I was like a piece of the puzzle that used to fit.

How could I explain to them what I was going through when I didn't even understand it myself? The fact is, I was in a horrible mood. After trying like hell to get released for rehabilitation into my own home, I had a hard time understanding why. Why was I so shitty to everyone? The problem was after surviving a stroke my emotional regulation was unpredictable. I felt that I was right all the time and destroyed anyone who dared to challenge me. There I was, working to recover, following my schedule to the T and profoundly emotional all the time. I wasn't mad at anyone in particular, but everyone caught the brunt of my anger just the same.

Of course I tried to see where I could give in a titch, but my stroke would not let me. I was losing control at every little thing that got my dander up, trying like hell to practice my mantras or anything to keep my cool. Without a doubt, had we been Japanese and could understand the language or living at home (Switzerland) where we understood the culture it, perhaps, would have been easier. Someone, a counselor or a therapist, might have explained to the kids and to my husband what they could expect from me and my outbursts.

I was a mama-lion and my little cubs needed protection...sometimes even from me. From my turmoil, I could see that they needed a shield for the times when they were vulnerable against me. Against my emotional outbursts, those times when I was raging and nothing could stop me from digging myself into a hole of words. I needed to give them the authority to stop me.

So, the word *candy cane*, with its bright, cheery overtones, took on a new meaning in our house. Now if someone shouts "candy cane," it doesn't mean that Santa is on his way. It's my shared code word with my family and their magical shield. It means that I should *STOP!* Breathe. Consider what is really important in my life, readjust, and go on. There isn't an after-effect. I've given my word that by shouting candy cane, the emotional outburst stops and the person who said it remains unscathed. We've given our family a way to control an uncontrollable situation.

Seth, being a big believer in talking things out, decided that it would help all of us if I wrote some "ground rules," things to discuss with them. So, in an effort to save myself and my family from me, I got straight to work. According to Seth, it would be beneficial to us all to know where we stood and some way to manage our expectations. This, for me, marked a significant step towards my mental recovery. It was the first time that I tried to alleviate anyone else's suffering.

With Seth, I typed up those guidelines, making sure that I took in all of our outlooks and needs, and printed them out. To this day, it is still sticky-tacked to the refrigerator door, signed by us all. It wasn't what it said as much as what it represented. It meant that we each were allowed to have our own point of view. What matters is how we react to each other.

Kids Rules:

1) You need to pick up your room
   a) Keep the laundry tidy
   b) Make your beds
   c) When you finish for the day please put your toys away
2) Because my free time will be cut back, we will put a message board on the refrigerator
   a) You can jot your things down during the day, for our dinner time discussion
      i) Things that happened during the day
      ii) Arguments that you can't figure out yourself
      iii) Playdates you want to arrange
   b) Mommie can use it the same way
      i) Things that happened during the day
      ii) Problems that I can see & hear, but I save for our dinner time discussion
3) Mommie promises to:
   a) Let nothing get in the way of dinner
   b) Discuss the things that you put on the board

    c)   Participate in therapy to have our lives back to normal
4)  Pappie promises to:
    a)   Let nothing get in the way of breakfast
    b)   Discuss the things with Mommy which she can't handle (from the board)
    c)   Be present as often as he can for bedtime

In the same vein, responsibilities like learning to cook dinner, folding clothes, and working out their problems by themselves have not only helped me, but they have also instilled a sense of partnership in our children. They've also been given the enormous, heavy task of learning how to call for help, should I fall victim to a re-stroke. That is something that I fervently hope they never experience. But they accepted the responsibility in stride.

Sure, they earn weekly pocket money for a job well done and, yes, the older two were given my old iPhones to make that emergency call, but I don't think, for one minute, that it is adequate compensation for all that they've gone through.

In order to give our children the power and the will to recover from my stroke, to make damn certain that we all do, we have had to feel the pain. And traipse on through. Through the shitty bits. The bits where I am screaming my head off. Through the uncertainty. And then, only then, through the reconstruction of our lives.

During these first months, my friends were instrumental in caring for me and my family. For the duration, although all I saw was a blurry mess, they kept watch over me. They not only were feeding us, they were looking out for me and my children, emotionally and physically. It would have been easier if we'd thrown me into a rehabilitation facility after my hospital stay, alleviating some of the stress that was bearing down on my precious family.

They enabled my children to get on with school. My kids didn't miss a single day. With them, my husband was able to keep (an altered) schedule at work. Despite his state of despair and with newly found responsibilities, he was able to put one foot in front of the other.

Katja had arranged for someone to bring us supper each weeknight. There was a constant stream of compassionate bodies shuffling through our front door, each bringing homemade delicacies with them. It was simply unbelievable. These people all had lives of their own, their own families to take care of. Yet, that didn't stop them from caring about me.

Suga was a great addition to our team. She allowed me and Johan safety. With her, we didn't stress about who would call the ambulance if I suffered a re-stroke or if I could walk to rehab. With Suga, I could stretch my range of abilities. She was my rock for those few weeks.

Still, emotionally, I was exhausted. The hours of therapy, the expectation, the fact that I couldn't make myself understood without a ton of effort were all getting to me. I was trying daily, pushing myself to the brink. Looking back, I can now see that this was a double-edged sword. My drive, my absolute hunger, was my impetus to recover, but also my limiting, merciless self-sabotage. I was always pushing pushing pushing, not giving myself credit for the achievements that I had accomplished.

I was super-sensitive and my go-to reaction was anger. Even the laundry machine eluded me. I can remember thinking, "It cannot be this hard. Which buttons do I push? Does the order matter?" I felt like it was taunting me. All these Japanese symbols were exasperating. I felt disgusted with Japan, as if the whole country were trying to provoke me.

The days ticked by, with me fighting myself and everyone who dared get in my way. I was getting better, slowly. Despite my foul-ups and even, dare I say, because of them, I was making progress. At this point, I started to see my indiscretions. I felt ashamed and worked even harder to minimize the damages that they caused.

The next challenge I had to face was going to the children's school for assembly. Lulu and Friso had been chosen to moderate it. It was a big deal for them, as they were announcing their classes' grand finale, The Exhibition. The Exhibition is a collaborative project that celebrates the end of primary school and it takes the better part of the last three months of the school year. I desperately wanted to go. It would take a lot of preparation on my part to feel fit enough to make it. So Suga and I had our work cut out for us!

Why that seemed like such a big deal, I now know. It was like doing everything for the first time, without any sense of myself. I was rebuilding everything from the ground up. I was learning how to communicate without my voice. I was learning how to walk without support. I was learning how to balance myself, literally and figuratively. It would cost me a great deal of time and energy to do this. And I only had a week.

It was a small school and everyone, at least it felt that way, knew about my stroke. I would be a focal point for all. I felt the pressure. I gathered my team, Suga, Katja, Gordana and Johan around me, cushioning me should I falter. They were solid. I felt like I could do anything with them by my side.

Katja, bless her, went ahead and saved our seats, in the back of the auditorium where we could easily escape, while

# (al)ONE

Gordana met me, Suga, and Johan at the bus stop. Slowly, we made our way in.

I walked in with my head facing towards the floor, not because I was embarrassed, but because it was the only way to will my feet to move. I knew people were looking at me, but I didn't care. I was solely concentrated on the stage, where my monkeys were seated. When I got to my seat, the enormity of the past seven weeks just hit. My heart quickened in speed. Seeing my two eldest standing before me, while surrounded by the love of my friends, was a sensation that I will remember for years to come.

I made little eye contact with anyone other than my children. It was like playing peek-a-boo with a baby. *If I can't see them, then they can't see me,* I was telling myself. My heart was racing. In fact, I had to check my heart rate several times on my new Apple Watch to manage my stress levels. I had done it. I got there in one piece.

Now what was happening? Someone was hurrying towards me. Oh! It can't be. I am not ready for this. She's coming. Don't look up. I kept my eyes down and fixed to the floor. It was too late. Someone was approaching me, I could feel it. As I looked up with despair, pleading with my eyes for this woman to be kind and go away, I realized that it was Gabby, my daughter's fifth grade teacher. Her warm and affectionate smile broke my icy exterior. She didn't even have to say anything, or maybe she did. All I knew is that when she enveloped me in her arms, I had found my first new friend. I have always admired Gabby with her smiley eyes, gorgeous hair and her brilliant fashion sense. Over time, I realized that what she did for me was to show how I could learn to trust again. And that is a gift that I will treasure forever.

I will never know what actually happened in that forty minutes, because my eyes were fixated on my children.

Those little survivors had me enraptured. They were going to do this. Hell, at that moment, I thought that we all could do this. I had no idea what else was going on, in the moment or with our future. It just felt good to be a normal mom, watching her children perform.

When it was winding down, Lorraine, the Head of School, swept down like a mama bird, protecting her young. Bless her cotton socks, she appeared out of nowhere, gave me a hug and discreetly ushered me out of the auditorium. I remember feeling sky-high at that point, like I could take on the world. Nothing could stop me. I remember not wanting to leave, although she was insisting.

Looking back, it was time to go. *Leave on a high note*, I remember myself always saying. This feeling of euphoria was caused by my emotional regulation issues. It was like I had no barometer, no way to measure which way the storm was going to blow. I was either high as a kite or feeling like dirt. There was no in between. Luckily Lorraine saved the day, or least saved me from myself.

I was reminded how life waits for no one. There we were, in a coffee shop by school, re-hashing each detail of the morning. If I were a fly on the wall, I would see just three school moms jibbering away. It could have been the same without me. For the moment, however, I was just thankful for the chance to be alive.

What I didn't realize is that there is a huge disparity between being alive and being fully in control of your life. By leaving the hospital, by not going to rehab and insisting that I go home, I was basically orphaning myself. While, on one hand, it was probably what helped improve my cognitive and reasoning abilities so quickly, I still find it the most difficult aspect about my recovery. I certainly wasn't up for the role of case manager.

For starters, you have to manage your therapists. Sounds easy, right? As a business woman, who is used to hiring, managing and, if it all goes terribly wrong, firing members of her team, I still found this incredibly difficult. My emotions were unreliable and my bullshit barometer could no longer be trusted. It was exacerbated by the "Japan factor." I only had access to a handful of English-speaking therapists and, although I found some great ones, there were others who took advantage of my situation. The thing is, I didn't know how to recover from a stroke and every English-speaking therapist said that they were "stroke specialists." I was completely at their mercy.

In my diminished capacity, I was not capable of managing the simple task of hiring. I'll always remember a physiotherapist that I eventually had to fire. He knew no boundaries and, presumptuously, spoke directly to my doctors without my consent. He was a shameless know-it-all without having the substance to back it up.

So, I got that totally wrong more than a few times. Though when I got it wrong, I could not simply fire them without conversing with Johan. For me, that was extremely difficult to process. In business, I would have a conversation with the person and manage their expectations. If you do this, then this will happen. In my mind, I knew what I wanted, but due to my aphasia, I couldn't articulate it. That made it problematic and I found it deeply troublesome to live this way.

Johan had the idea that more was better. For instance, he found two speech therapists for me to try. Considering that we were living in Japan, I was lucky. So, I began with both of them. After some time, it became abundantly clear that Seth was a better fit for me. With Seth, I could focus on what was supremely important to me, my writing. We were able to incorporate everything that was important for me to relearn into that basic function.

The other therapist insisted that we go through the motions of learning her way. She would flash cards at me, insisting that I should know the word. When I inevitably could not say the words or describe the situation correctly, she would say, "'Wrong!" She treated me like a second grader. She seriously diminished my self-worth and made me feel ashamed of myself. For having a stroke??

However, due to my aphasia and my reduced cognitive abilities, I could not convince Johan that she was not right for me. I simply would shout that it wasn't working, but in my heart I just wanted him to understand me. I willed him to understand.

He was just worried that if something happened with Seth, that I would be left with no one. I fully agreed with Johan, however just because something scares you is no reason to make up your mind. For me, Seth represents much more than a speech therapist. If something happens to him, I would be heartbroken. He understands what I am going through and all of my weird, wacky, and sometimes aggressive behaviors. He's giving of himself and his mind. He's strong and sensitive at the same time. He's been there, where I am, suffering a brain injury and clawing like mad at anything, everything, to get yourself back again.

So, I felt in my heart that I had to let the other therapist go. Thankfully I had Suga to watch my back, stick up for me, and sort my words out. She was there every day and we trusted her implicitly. She could fill in the blanks when I was struggling. She was like no one that I have had the pleasure to meet, always listening. The long, arduous task of convincing Johan began. He was adamant. He didn't want to get rid of the other speech therapist. No matter how much I despised working with her, he thought keeping her was for my own good.

I still remember how small I felt. It was the same feeling that I experienced when my parents made me do something that I didn't want to do. But in some parts of my mind, I began to question my judgement. Was I wrong? What if something happened to Seth? Then where would I be? My heart knew the answers. But could I trust my heart? So, we plodded on in a state of limbo. As we planned on escaping to Switzerland for the summer, I plotted my escape from her. I would see her until we left and simply not tell her when we returned to Japan. Just like an impish child.

Had I had the ability to reason with him, I would have been able to explain that I was spending a minimum of two hours per day in speech therapy already. A second therapist meant that I was adding an additional hour per day. That was too much, even for someone motivated like me.

Finding an occupational therapist was another story. After leaving the hospital, where I had access to a therapist most days, Johan found two English-speaking therapists to interview. So, armed with Suga, we did just that. What I know now, that I didn't know then, is that you have to be very specific on who you are interviewing. What is their background? What is their approach, and are they open to new therapies or new methods of training?

In talking to both of the therapists, I could tell that they were absolutely different. Age made no difference to me and I could imagine myself being treated by the young, too-cool-for-school therapist. However, it became apparent that she was a complete narcissist.

She took two sessions to fill out her "form," which focused on ridiculous questions, asked in a condescending voice. I took a mean disliking to her. The most I got from our meetings was the laughable advice that, "Did your doctor tell you that while you are on antiplatelets, you shouldn't shave your legs?" Oh my God!

The other, older, therapist was warm and we connected instantly. Without hesitation, she asked me what I wanted to do with my affected arm (play tennis, cook, write and take pictures) so we dug in and that's where we started. It was clear that she'd been around the block with stroke survivors and took a practical approach to finding what motivates them to recover.

In fact, she asked to see my camera and gave me a superb pointer, to put a velcro sticky on the shutter button so I could feel it. I still use it to this day. She asked me to go grab my tennis racket and there we stood, just holding it. It felt so good.

In the end, when you know, you know. However, if you can't get the words to come out, you could be stuck with a shameless know-it-all or someone who has something to prove. If I had to do it all over again, here is the list of questions that I came up with to suss out whether a therapist is right for me before hiring them. Even if you cannot find your words.

Is their personality one that you can connect with?

What is their background?

What is their approach and are they open to new therapies or new methods of training?

What are their hopes and outcomes they expect for you?

Does this match your expectations?

How will we set goals and measure them?

*If you want to download these questions, you can find them on my website: www.staciebroek.com Click "Free Tools" in the main menu.*

Those early days were painfully monotonous. I could not walk unaided. I couldn't stand by myself. I couldn't even run the flipping washing machine. I was beginning to feel sick of myself. If going from one therapist to another doesn't get to you, talking about it sure does. Practically speaking, the conversation about every banal detail of my life and who "is taking care of me" is one that I would rather do without. What makes it more troublesome is the fact that we were discussing my life as if we were discussing a newborn baby. It managed to be both humiliating and boring.

By the end of my first month at home, I felt like I was riding an emotional roller coaster. And I wanted off. I found it exasperating to be treated like a child and just wanted the chance to spread my wings a little bit further.

The chance finally came when Johan, who plays tennis each weekend morning, agreed to let me stay by myself, with the children and without Suga, for those two hours. However, for all my pleading it turned out that, perhaps, I wasn't ready. As I sat on the couch with the children, I noticed that I couldn't feel my right leg. Now, it wasn't any more numb than it had been since my stroke, but the panic of re-stroke, and the fear of having it in front of the children, got the better of me.

We ended up taking a trip to the Emergency Room that day.

All of the frustration, all of the anxious moments, were taking a toll on our marriage. We had been married for sixteen years before my stroke. Long enough to have experienced pure joy with our three children. Long enough to have experienced the devastating aftermath of loss. If anything would break us apart, we both knew that it could be this.

Talking, even during the times when all we wanted to do was to block it out, became paramount. Unfortunately, talking was extremely hard for us, as we both have our deficiencies in this area.

# CHAPTER 10
## Finding the New Norm
*Weeks 9 - 18: When you are up… there's no way to go but down?*

Little by little, I gained a broader sense of myself, and we carved out a new normal. I was ready to take on more. I believed that I would not fully recover without pushing myself. Whether or not that's true, I cannot say. However, it was definitely what got me through those first few weeks at home. It was as if I were a slippery teenager, pushing my limits against my parents' will and behind their backs.

I embraced my new morning routine. It was very different from what I was used to. Previously, I had been the one to rush the children along, fighting like a madwoman to get them on the bus on time. After my stroke, when Johan took over my duties, it felt like a cinch. I would wake up, stretch for a few minutes and get ready to go while listening to my favorite playlist. This was also therapeutic, as music is known to have calming qualities;

by listening to my faves, over and over again, I was retraining my brain.

After my musical dance-it-out-sesh, Johan would very sweetly serve me breakfast. I ate the same thing every day: two rye crackers and Dutch cheese that my father-in-law sent over from Holland. At the precise moment I was finished, Suga was at the door to take me to PT. In those days, we had to take a taxi, although it was a short one point one kilometers from our apartment, because my exhaustion level would rise quickly and my endurance would wane. I found it taxing to be late, which would inevitably happen, if I allowed myself to walk.

I had a great PT, Chris, who was motivating, always in a great mood, and made me laugh every morning with yet another of his dad's jokes. I was always motivated to see Chris. He treated me as if there wasn't anything wrong with me, making me count aloud as I went through the reps of my exercises. That was a cause for more giggles, as I couldn't keep track of the numbers at all. What comes after five? Damned if I knew! While that wouldn't be mind-boggling for someone who hadn't just suffered a stroke, it was wildly complex for me.

Chris also knew that in my condition, I couldn't handle a lot of stress or noise, due to my sensory integration issues. I could not filter out sounds that my brain didn't need. So when the Saturday morning boxing class was on for instance, not wanting to push me but in effort to get me used to the noise, he would speak very gently to me and watch carefully for any sign that I'd had enough.

I remember one time a panicky feeling crept over me, ten minutes into my session. Sometimes the stress of doing a new exercise, moving my body in a particular way that was suddenly foreign to me, combined with my depleted trust in my body, would cause my emotional control to dither. It was like, all of a sudden, I was standing alone on a peak and with my next breath I would fall off, plummeting into a gorge of blackness.

Chris didn't miss a beat. He took me by the hand, back to his office, and told me that it was going to be okay. That I could talk to him. I could scream at him. He knew that it was all too much for me at that very point.

Chris was also huge in boosting my confidence and my ability to socialize, because he was young, perceptive, and sure, almost to the point of cheekiness. He made me feel like it was okay to not be able to spit out my words. In fact, we would laugh at my aphasia sometimes. His favorite line was, "Jeez, did you have a stroke or something?" While that wouldn't work for everyone, it did for me, and I had to laugh. Humor, mixed with hard work, is what got me through those days.

After each PT session, rain or shine, Suga and I would walk back home, stopping for coffee and enjoying life. We were often joined by Katja or another one of my dear friends. In my heart I knew that Suga could not stay forever, in fact I didn't want her to by this point. I was searching for the security that she provided me, but without her physically being there. Suga was the one who experienced so many firsts with me.

For example, the first time I visited a supermarket. We only went in to buy milk. The noises, the copious amounts of food, the throngs of people were overpowering. As we got to the dairy aisle, I began to feel an incessant urge to disappear, to be swallowed whole by the market. I threw money at Suga, with barely an apology, leaving her to buy the milk. And then, when I realized that I would have to navigate the way out without her, I grabbed her arm in a plea to get me out. Without the milk.

The first time I went for a manicure. Suga was by my side. In my mind she could have gone for a coffee while I was pampered but, ever the professional, she sat right by my side in the waiting room. Annoyingly. She said something in Japanese to my manicurist, presumably about my condition, and it made me seethe. Of course I wanted to be protected and it was her job, but something about it really irked me. Instead of enjoying the treatment, I was doing a slow burn.

The first time I took the train. I was filled with dread. The escalators were so steep I thought I would tip backwards, and the millions of people, all clambering to push their way into the train car, were frightening. Suga held out her hand for me, as if to say "we can do this," so I carried on with trepidation. As the train boomed towards us, I was completely focused on my balance. Luckily, we got on, but didn't get seats. We faced the perilous predicament of hanging on the hand rails. I made it halfway to our destination. After that trip, Suga bought me a handicapped "mark," denoting people that need special attention with their emergency details on the back, that I started wearing on my bag.

Or the first time I rode the bus. Armed with my new "mark" I thought it would be significantly easier to ride the bus; however it was the first time I felt ashamed of my disabilities. Suga and I climbed on board a full bus and stood on the aisle of handicapped seats, me displaying my "mark." When no one offered me their seat, Suga spoke in Japanese to an able bodied gentleman, who proceeded to look me up and down in disdain before completely blanking me. Suga was in shock. Was he judging me because I didn't look handicapped? Or was it that I was foreign? Or both? Whatever the reason, I was filled with embarrassment.

# (al)ONE

To find the security to replace Suga took me a very long time.

My first trip to the hair salon with Johan took us six hours and a lot of stress. I felt depleted from making our way across town, which isn't something to be taken lightly because we were living in the center of Tokyo, rehearsing what I would say to my stylist (because needless to say Johan would for sure get it wrong!) and the anxiety of tipping my head back to the sink. I had a hard time believing that this was something I considered worth it just a few short months ago. We had planned to celebrate this milestone with a drink, just the two of us. However, after the long afternoon, the emotions and the incessant need to lie down got the better of me. I just couldn't muster up the strength.

I am a big "what-if" girl. What if I have a re-stroke? What if I am alone with the children and they don't know what to do? I was drowning in "what-ifs." The trust that I had in my body, that I had built over the course of my forty-six years on earth, trust that I could walk and talk, that I could think my way out of a sticky spot, had been rudely and abruptly taken from me. What was put in its place was a frightened, raging beast of a woman. I felt very alone.

Fortunately, by this time, I had forged a relationship with Seth and, together, we set out to banish the boogeymen from rearing their ugly heads. He taught me to look at the worst-case scenario in all that I was afraid of. We tore apart every bit, every nook, of those dark ghosts that were haunting me. What we built in their place were strategies that I could quickly implement when I was in a downward spiral.

For instance, one of my biggest worries was if I suffered a re-stroke, how would I notify my family and what would they do? So, for twenty bucks, I installed a wireless doorbell system that enabled me to hit a buzzer anytime that I felt insecure, or strokey. I could take a bath and feel secure that someone would come when I buzzed. I could safely fall asleep knowing that I only had to press my buzzer if something wasn't right.

Then, Johan wrote out all of the emergency numbers on a chart and glued it to the refrigerator, with my history, in English and Japanese. No matter when I suffered a theoretical re-stroke, if I was at home, I would be taken care of.

Suddenly, the uncontrollable situation seemed to be more *controlled*. It wasn't that I considered the problem solved, but the steps we took enabled me to manage my fear. The solutions were life-giving, or at least emotionally liberating. Finally, I could beat the demons at their own game!

In fact, a good plan, not only for the creepy bits, but for everything that I encountered, is what got me through those days. Brushing my teeth and doing my mouth exercises (to work on the drooping side of my mouth) happened at eight o'clock each morning and at nine o'clock each night, without qualm or fail. Time interacting with the children happened at five o'clock on the dot each evening.

I could not have dreamt of becoming so militant in my approach, of becoming my own cheerleader and my own case manager all wrapped up in a nice stroke-survivor package.

My children were aces at giving me the time that I needed. We had the rules taped to the refrigerator and we all were emphatic about adhering to them, but it wasn't a normal situation at all. They couldn't run to me when they got off the school bus, for instance, or tattletale on one another. Everything had to be put on hold until five o'clock. I was all theirs for the next hour and forty-five minutes, and then, back to my therapies.

We didn't hold anything back from the children. They knew that in order for me to get better, they had to keep up their end of the bargain. I knew that I couldn't take care of them, or instantly slide back into my role as their mother. I found it quite easy to split my life into these divided roles. I couldn't handle anything more.

It was completely natural, once the pause button of my life had been hit by my stroke, to find joy in napping or to practice my handwriting with journaling, neither of which I did before. Artistically, my passions of writing, cooking and taking pictures had been liberated. I was a writer before. If I didn't write, I wouldn't make money. If I didn't cook dinner, my children would go hungry. Now, I could indulge my creative juices because of and alongside my stroke. To say that I found joy in my stroke is pushing it, but I found that there were nevertheless many joyful facets of my recovery. Unbeknownst to me, I was working towards a holistic approach to my recovery, and also my life.

All of these activities, like sitting with the children or working with Seth, took energy from my brain, from me. In just twelve short weeks, I went from not being able to get myself from point A to B without a wheelchair, to walking the distance from PT all the way to my house. The neurons were on fire and my poor brain, while trying like mad to take all of the influences in, was utterly exhausted.

At this time I was doing two hours of speech and language therapy with Seth, one hour every other day with the other speech therapist, an hour of PT and an hour every other day of OT. That is a hell of a lot of learning. It didn't leave me a lot of time to figure out things like ordering on-line, for instance.

I will never forget the first time, post-stroke, trying to order my contact lenses. My memory failed me as to where I ordered them from. I knew that it was an optician on the Bahnhofstrasse in Zürich, but where? I could have simply searched for clues in my email inbox like "contact order" or "optik" or "brillen," but cognitively I was blocked.

At that point, however, my phone was used to call in or out. Although I knew that it once was utilized in a significantly more handy way, I could not grasp what it was. My computer's sole purpose was to have my virtual meeting with Seth, every day. I was unable to do or see more with it. I couldn't connect the dots. It was madly frustrating to me to forget the name of the optician. I had ordered my lenses from the same place for several years.

Thinking that I was clever, I asked Suga to pull up a map of the Bahnhofstrasse on her phone and there we sat, all afternoon, searching for the place. Then, when I thought I had surely found it, I asked Johan to send them an email on my behalf. When he did, they politely told him that they didn't have a Stacie Broek as a patient. Back to the drawing board.

The fight with my daily life, or just realizing what my daily life could or should look like, was exhausting. Putting my contacts in cost me about twenty minutes per day, and that was only if my right hand would play along. Washing my hair took a lot of patience, practice, and inner confidence. Because I could not keep my balance long enough to wash and condition my hair standing up in the shower, I knelt down on the bathroom floor and put my head under the spigot. Each time, this caused great fear for my carotid artery, which was not yet healed. The world would spin as I washed it and all I had to draw on was that here, in this moment, I was doing everything to keep myself safe.

To rebuild the trust, of my body, my mind, and of my emotions, was a slow and gradual process, not only for me but for Johan as well. Johan had his own demons creeping up on him. He perhaps would have liked to be his feel-good self, and Suga let him, but the more I pushed her away, the more he realized that he was fighting an uphill battle. Johan was worried about me. He knows that I am a headstrong woman and I fight for everything I believe in. He was very concerned that by warding off Suga, I was not doing myself any favors. He was afraid of losing his freedom, and the responsibility of caring for me was overwhelming.

We were positively petrified of doing this without her. However, six weeks after my homecoming and twelve weeks after my stroke, it was time to say goodbye to Suga, and to all the security that her presence had brought us.

I knew that we had taken all the precautions that we could have thought of, all systems were in place. Just the same, Johan took some afternoons off here and there just to keep me company, or more likely to check in on me. One afternoon, we walked to Starbucks to grab coffee. We were planning on sitting there, in the sunshine, and working for the afternoon. Oddly, Johan's computer couldn't connect to the internet and he needed to move to another restaurant. As I still had a full cup, he acquiesced to my cries to be left alone, finish my coffee and to walk the length of a city block, to the next restaurant. I felt so free!

In that moment, from the outside, I was just a girl sunning herself. On the inside, however, I was bursting with happiness. I can still remember what I was wearing that day, the day when I first was able to walk alone in Tokyo. Without Suga. Without Johan. All aIone, for a whole city block.

I kept pushing my limits, and those of Johan as well; not because I meant to, but because I didn't see any other way. Something instinctive was driving me. Some days were not as successful as this one was. For instance, the time when I was at home alone and I couldn't catch my breath. It felt as if my pulse was drumming in my ears. I was scared. Instinctively I knew that it was just a panic attack, but something else was driving me. The fear was palpable. I had to call Johan in the office because my heart was racing a mile a minute. He left immediately, never putting the phone down, leaving his computer and jacket, talking to me gently while speeding home in a taxi.

Or the day that I had a street fight with a bunch of university girls. I was with Johan and we were enjoying our new favorite frozen banana juice from the shop in the village, smug with ourselves for playing hooky for the afternoon. Johan was pushing his bicycle and I was strolling next to him, chatting happily about one thing or another, both of us knee-deep in conversation.

I shudder and close my eyes when I think about the ugly behavior that surfaced in me during our stroll when a group of young women came walking our way. My reaction was vile. It ran the gamut from pure annoyance, to self-righteous indignation, to "I was here first, now step aside!"

When we saw the ladies coming, en masse, Johan naturally wheeled his bicycle over to the other side of the street to let them pass. I, on the other hand, didn't even think about getting out of their way. I thought they were wenches by assuming that I would get out of their way. They were walking side-by-side, in twos, not leaving enough room for me to pass! I made all of those girls pass me in a single file. I could only imagine what they were thinking as they looked up at this mad woman. That's when I started yelling. I began screaming about the girls, the fact that they were happy, the sunshine, the rain, my stupid lack of communication skills, the heat, what I had for breakfast, Japan, Switzerland, and on and on it went. I was shouting about everything and anything. To be blunt, I lost my shit. I embarrassed Johan and, ultimately, myself.

Before my stroke, I would like to think that I had a dimmer switch to help guide me. When emotional, my dimmer switch turned on the adrenaline full blast during a deserving event, like an intruder in my house, and it could dial it way back to a catty remark when encountering that sea of ladies on the sidewalk. After, it seemed as if my dimmer switch had turned into a great big button labeled "You want your emotion? Here, have it all!" And it ignites some irrational monster inside me in response to every situation, blocking me from other choices.

Since my stroke, Seth explained that my brain has problems with emotional regulation. So the message is sent by my lower brain for processing and where I used to have a dimmer switch, to decide what actions I'm going to take, what comes back is a convoluted mixed message: "Stand your ground at all costs! Don't let the ladies, or anyone, stop you!" It actually doesn't matter what my brain is processing; if it sees red, then it's game over. My emotional filter has been reduced to zero.

I have the emotional stigma that plays with my mind as well. As good as it felt at the time, I knew that it was not right to yell at the girls. Like an adult-turned-toddler, I have to retrain every part of my brain, from emotional regulation to balancing. I don't know which is harder, dealing with the fact that I am a grown woman who yells unfairly at people or relearning to ride my bike. The cognitive, emotional, and physical casualties are all-encompassing and it's very hard to see them separately. The world reacts to my strokey symptoms like trying to tip a waiter, riding a bike or yelling at the ladies very differently too. It runs the gamut from "ah, how sweet" to pure annoyance to "OMG she's losing her shit." From my perspective, it's all shit.

You see, stroke recovery is not visceral to others. You see only what you want to see. However, for the survivors, we don't have that luxury. I cannot expect anything other than my broken, battered, candid self each time. I cannot accommodate you.

Riding my bike, previously the easiest and most practical way to navigate the city, was utterly impossible for me in the earlier days of my recovery. I will never forget the first time that I picked it up, after my stroke. Johan and Cleo were there with me, rooting me on. I was a nervous wreck. Squidge was riding easily and without the enormous effort that I mentally and physically had to put in.

She was my biggest cheerleader, although her racing around me in loops was about to do my head in. At some point, when I stirred up enough courage to actually go, she was so excited for me that she got too close and our wheels interlocked. Boy, that was scary.

Little by little, I gained confidence and balance to the point where I could ride further and, at some point, alone. The fact that I rode my bike to school, to lunch, to pick up groceries– these were all milestones. I will never forget the first time I rode my bike all the way to lunch with my sweet friend, Michelle. I was like a child when you first took off her training wheels. I was teetering down the sidewalk, silently begging people to make way. As I parked my bike outside the restaurant I might have silently prayed that it would get stolen so I didn't have to ride it back. That wobbly feeling could only be countered by my extreme determination.

Because my carotid artery was not healed, I was vehemently following all of my doctors' orders and going for my monthly MRIs. I didn't mind going to them, although it took me the better part of a day each time. I equated this feeling with my pregnancies. The times I felt safest were always the days following a scan. I could pacify my wild imagination with the fact that our baby was safe and had a strong heartbeat, until the next time. Likewise, I could see my artery, and its vulnerable section, on the images captured by my Magnetic Resonance Angiography (MRA - an MRA is a technique used to capture images of blood vessels). It was weirdly comforting to me.

My doctors in Japan are some of the most accomplished people I will ever have the pleasure to meet. They not only saved my life by quickly pulling a team together and fearlessly trying a surgery that had only been performed ten times in Japan, they took care of me afterwards. The cultural difference between us was, sometimes, shocking. I was younger than most stroke patients. I didn't blindly accept what they said unless it also rang true in my ears. I questioned things. And when I didn't like what they were telling me, I sought out my own truth.

Because of the fact that they knew so little about my condition and alongside the perception that the doctor knows best, we didn't always understand one another. Persistence on both of our parts played a huge role. As they, with their strict formalities, grudgingly accepted the brash American woman who definitely said what she thinks and the transformations I was making, we slowly formed a bond that wasn't typical.

I came prepared for every one of those follow-up MRIs with the doctor who had been assigned to my case. In my mind, it wasn't a perfect match. For one thing, he didn't have a strong grasp of the English language.

This time, on my second visit after leaving the hospital, I asked him what happens next. I knew that my carotid artery was not healed, but what was the plan? Without thinking, he simply said that if it wasn't healed within a year of my stroke they would perform another angiogram to see what the real situation was. At that time, I could not distinguish whether it was a language barrier or the simple truth. For me, it didn't matter. My doctor said it, so it felt very real.

Culturally, in Japan, the doctor is all-knowing. I suspect that no one had ever dared to ask this question. As an American, I wouldn't dream of not asking. I was an exceptional case, the eleventh person in all of Japan to have this surgery; he could have, and should have told me that he would consult with his colleagues and get back to me.

Another angiogram felt much like a conviction. Although it is the most accurate way to see the situation, by sticking a microscopic camera from my groin to my neck, it is a very invasive procedure when you have a damaged and turbulent carotid artery wall. I was stunned. I couldn't think of the other questions that I wanted to ask. It all went black. It was the first time that I felt truly mortal. And remember, my post-stroke brain didn't know colors. Everything was either black or white. Nothing in between. I arrived at that appointment alive and I was leaving with a death sentence. I left with a heavy heart and a very big cloud hanging over my shoulders.

I couldn't shake his words off. The last time I was taken for this procedure, I was in the hospital for six weeks, had suffered a stroke and found out that the only thing that saved me was a risky operation that could have gone either way. I was triggered by the thought that I could have died in the operation, or afterwards, and I was completely unaware of what was happening to me. Subsequently, I have had to struggle to climb out of the abyss that was my life. With that struggle came the understanding that life was perilous and should not be taken for granted. For me, I could picture myself dying in a year from this very procedure.

I was spinning from one black thought to another. I could not accept this! On some level I knew that his answer must be false, a mismatch of languages or words. I couldn't imagine the doctors wanting to risk my safety. I was shaken.

In talking about it with Seth, we explored what I was most worried about, the real-life implications. The fear was almost tangible. I could smell it. With every beat of my heart, I could feel it pulsing in my veins. However, this I was able to endure. I thought that I could manage my anxieties. What I was most scared about was preparing my children for the death of their mother and my husband for the death of his wife.

The thought of leaving my children, my husband, was more than I could bear. In an effort to control yet another uncontrollable situation, Seth suggested that I make videos for them. So I began, with my iPhone and my words, slowly recording daily life as well as milestones in their lives. I am poignantly aware of the strength that this gave me. After struggling to set-up the camera correctly on the selfie-stick, after seeing my worn face in the camera's lens and after stammering thru, sometimes bursting into tears throughout my narration, I managed this gut-wrenching task. And, somehow, I drew power from it.

Seth and I then made a list of questions that I was going to ask at my follow-up appointment which I scheduled for the end of the week with the department head, my doctor's boss. In hindsight, I was devising a battle plan to fight the demons in my head. I coveted the logic, the reasons why.

I was ready to understand. In fact, I needed it. I went to that appointment armed with my questions and open to all possibilities.

I didn't get the answers I would have liked at that appointment. I was expecting an answer along the lines of "Based on the procedure we performed and the circumstances such as your age, condition and first weeks of recovery, we suspect that in X amount of months (years?) your artery will be healed." But because my situation was so new to the doctors, in fact new to everyone, they just didn't have the answers. Dr. Ichi-san looked at me very seriously. He could see the pain in my eyes. He replied to my question "What happens next?" with extreme care. He said that, while they've never been in this particular situation, he suggested a conservative approach. If my artery did not heal itself within three years then, and only then, would they consider the invasive angiogram procedure. I wanted to kiss him.

I also learned that I could fly home to Switzerland for vacation that summer. So, I decided to take matters into my own hands. I was going to get second, third, and even fourth opinions in Zürich, from doctors whose culture and language I understood. So armed with Johan and his mighty Rolodex we began another search, this time for neurosurgeons in Zürich.

In planning for the trip, I requested my hospital records from my doctor. At the appointed time, I returned to the hospital to pick them up. I thought that this would be an easy breeze-in, breeze-out situation, but I had to sit down with my doctor. The first one. The one that I was beginning to lose trust in. I tried to use the appointment to my advantage by asking if he had any suggestions for the long plane ride home. I was thinking along the lines of strategies to help me avoid a stroke or what position Johan could put me in if I had a stroke. I asked "What can we do if I have a re-stroke?" And he answered, "Call a doctor." Jesus. At thirty thousand feet. Call a doctor. Was this a bad joke? Was it his poor language skills? Does it even matter?

Surviving a stroke is hard enough without having to second-guess, recalculate, and question every nook and cranny. I was driven by the hope that we could find a sparring partner in Zürich because the problem with being an orphan of the stroke system is that you rarely have anyone to bounce ideas and strategies off of. I took this as the opportunity to find just that. I had extremely high hopes.

Four short months, sixteen weeks, after surviving the worst, most terrifying ordeal that I have ever experienced, I was facing guilt mixed with anticipation. Guilt, because I was very aware that I harbored condescending thoughts about the doctors who had saved my life. Anticipation, because I was about to act on my doubts. This duality caused many emotions. It was the first time I realized how fortunate I was. Many people who had suffered what I had would not be able to rise up against their doctors, their caretakers, and their own abilities.

I started to figure out that it wasn't only I who was suffering. It was the first time that I realized I wasn't alone. I had people, support groups and friends who were also suffering, not from a stroke perhaps, but from their own traumas. I found it tricky to navigate this revelation, though. Why did I survive? It was also the first time that I realized that it's okay to ask for help.

Kara's visit came at precisely the right time, although I had a hard time recognizing it. I couldn't see the situation clearly. I was extremely focused on the end of the school year and our subsequent trip to Switzerland. I found it burdensome to wrap my head around more. Reservations about her visit crept into my mind. How would I show her around Tokyo? Would I have to cook dinner for her? I was hung up on these ridiculous thoughts. Of course she had no such expectations, but in my mind they were real and omnipresent. She only wanted to hug me and see for herself the wreckage that my stroke had caused.

Upon her arrival, I met her at her hotel. It was the longest embrace ever. Over the next few days we spoke about everything. A very intuitive woman, Kara asked me what I was afraid of. I admitted to her that my inability to break down my trip to Switzerland into manageable pieces was daunting and about to do my head in. The list of doctors, the plane ride and packing were all too confusing to me. I was not able to concentrate on one thing at a time, complete it and then cross it off the list. I was intimidated to make a simple packing list, for instance. My hand was not able to write. I couldn't count or spell. I couldn't mentally categorize outerwear from shoes. Kara was kind. She asked me if she could help and I accepted her offer.

After making my packing list for Switzerland and helping me pack the kids and myself, she disappeared, with a promise that if I needed her to come back in the fall I only had to say the word.

The last day of school rolled around. As I was boarding my flight to Switzerland, I couldn't help the thoughts that were whirling around in my brain. I've had to adapt to my fair share of disappointments in life. I've had to fight the feeling that I was robbed of many things that should be taken for granted. At a young age, I was the unlucky one who suffered something so incredibly rare that the only solution was a surgery performed only ten times. However, I've had loads of luck within my unluckiness. Everything from the fact that there was a team of doctors to pull that rare surgery off, to having a kind-hearted friend to pack for me, is proof of that.

So how does a woman without her voice accomplish things? It turns out that mine was never lost in the first place. She was right here, waiting for me all along.

# CHAPTER 11
## The Golden Nugget of Opportunity
### *Weeks 18 - 26: Summertime and the Livin' Is(n't) Easy.*

Abruptly, all of the comforts of home seemed to disappear, albeit in an expected way.

One minute you have your rhythm, which is very important to a person suffering from a neurological dysfunction, and then summertime rolls in with its bright and shiny façade.

To say I was scared of that first flight would be a massive understatement. I actually asked my doctor to prescribe something to help take the edge off, but once on the plane I was too scared to take those pills. On some level, and I'll admit that it's not rational, I am scared of anesthetizing my physical pains or my emotional senses. It's the same reason why I abstain from taking an ibuprofen for a headache and the same reason why I need to feel my emotions, even if they are painful.

The search to find myself again cannot be clouded with drugs or magical potions that allow me to hide. I need to search truthfully, feel everything, and learn to trust again.

My doctor had done his best to explain that flying does not bring on strokes, that as long as I didn't scrunch up my neck that he could not see a problem with us going back home. That didn't quash our fears. The minute we were buckled into our seats Johan and I exchanged looks of doubt and apprehension. We'd been through enough.

Preparing for and enduring the flight was a trial, but I was flooded with emotions at the other end of that twelve-hour plane journey. It wasn't just that I'd taken another step on the steep recovery ladder. Flying–or surviving it– represented so much more than just a flight from Tokyo to Zürich. I had moved the needle up a notch with a scary step like taking a flight. I had the power. And it felt good. I gained momentum by reaching as far as I could, leaping from one rung of the ladder to the next and feeling the joy of my accomplishments.

I don't know if it was the excitement of achievement or the warm feeling of home, but when we rolled up to our house in Switzerland I felt like I was soaring. My feet didn't touch the ground anymore. Johan's parents were there to greet us with hugs and, as we sat in the garden and watched the children play until sunset, I had a moment of pure euphoria. At that moment, I wasn't thinking about all the therapies, all of the work I had to do. It was a moment of pure elation, to spend the summer in Switzerland.

I had taken the week off from my therapies, as we had scheduled appointments for second opinions. We were introduced through Maria to her network of doctors, and by my friend Anita, who'd lost her husband to brain cancer, to hers.

As we drove down from the mountains to my first appointment, I could feel my body tensing again. This was the moment of truth, where I would be judged in a very clinical manner by the Swiss doctors on how the Japanese doctors performed the surgery. Through no fault of my own, it felt like I was on trial, waiting for judgment. I couldn't chase the scary thoughts from my consciousness. I could picture the Swiss doctors telling me that I only had X months to live or that my stent needed to be replaced, both of which sent me into a downward spiral.

It was sweltering hot in the city that summer. I remember having those doctors' appointments, with the kids in tow, and retiring by the lake in the evenings to fight the abnormally hot summer nights. Nothing could stop me from thinking the worst. My kids would drown in the lake and I could not save them. I would suffer a second stroke. My husband would have no one. Spiral. Spiral.

After the third opinion confirming that yes, my Japanese doctors had excelled at placing the stent and yes, I could, with a copious amount of work, get my life back, I began to calm down. In fact, the hospital where I got that third opinion was precisely the hospital where the procedure to place a stent in the wall of a redundant carotid artery was developed in the first place. So, I thought that they ought to know best.

I believed in this hospital and the neurosurgeons there. Finally, I had a team of doctors that I could communicate effectively with. That being said, the information that they delivered to me was sometimes confusing and contradictory. For instance, they told me that I could do everything except play tennis, that I should not let my stroke or my carotid artery stop me. On the other hand, after an ultrasound to compare the blood flow to my brain on my left side with my right side, they said that it was "disproportionate." I had no idea what that meant. Neither did they.

To make sense of this, my doctor told me of a newer and less-frequently used type of MRI which provides data on the blood flow rate in vessels of the brain. It can measure how much blood is flowing, how fast it's moving, and in which direction. I was scheduled for a NOVA MRI later that summer; in the meantime, I was told to continue working towards recovery.

I'd like to think that I handled myself honestly and appropriately in the doctor's office. I told him that I'd lost fifteen kilograms because food didn't usually appeal to me. I could muster one proper meal a day and that was only if the meal really grabbed my attention. The doctor suggested antidepressants.

We asked how long my recovery would take, given the severity of my stroke, my accomplishments thus far, and my obvious deficits. He answered, "There's no way to tell."

I showed him my foot, which was cramped into a ball. He diagnosed this as a chronic Babinski reflex and suggested that I visit their PT to be fitted for a Nordic Neuro Incedo. I didn't have any idea what that was. And he did little to help me understand.

I began to regress, the old fears seeping in. The doctor was treating me as if I were a number. He wasn't listening! Antidepressants? What? I politely told him that I was not willing to take even an ibuprofen for a headache. I know that every stroke is different and every patient is different. But what can a stroke patient from a dissected carotid artery, who is working at least three to five hours each day, expect? A full recovery? Less than that? I couldn't communicate with him! It was utterly devastating to hear the same stock answers that imagined he gave to everyone else. I had so many hopes, and they were all quashed. So I gave up.

What I didn't show him was my hand, which I could not use to put in my contacts. Or my running nose, which I could not feel. Or my prefabricated answers to general questions, which were well-rehearsed. He only wanted to see what he wanted to see. There was no use reaching out.

Somehow, I left the doctor's office feeling like unless you have survived a stroke, you cannot possibly know what it entails or the difficulties it leaves you with. Because surviving this type of stroke is so rare, there is a void of information about the recovery process. I felt like I belonged in a very distinctive group, but a sense of loss enveloped me when I realized that I was treated like I was a sheer number.

Despite this, the trip to Zürich was magical in some ways. On a return trip to our old neighborhood, I actually drove for the first time since my stroke. Carefully and calmly I tackled that hurdle, surrounded by my family. I equate driving with freedom and all things that we, as adults, have earned. To be separated from that had been painful in a deep way.

I also found strength where I least expected it. After hearing through the grapevine that I had survived a stroke, an ex-colleague, Annette, got in touch, and we met for breakfast in Zürich. I wouldn't have blamed her for looking the other way because that's what we, as humans, tend to do. Still, she was there, despite our differences, because she thought she could help me. I was simply overwhelmed with gratitude. She introduced me to the world of essential oils; after hearing my lingering symptoms, put together two blends, one for my brain and one for my muscles.

Annette, with her knowledge of and passion for essential oils, intrigued me. I'd been working for nearly half a year and no one had introduced the concept of non-medical treatments. I felt incredibly lucky to have her in my life. As I saw it, rubbing the oils on my temples for my brain and down my leg to my foot might help, and it smelled great! Where was the downside? It was then that I began to develop my big-picture approach to my recovery. If it feels right, it doesn't need a further explanation. I began thinking, if a treatment or a technique brings me, at least for a moment, any physical, sensory, intellectual, emotional, social or spiritual relief, I was going to do it! I was open to trying anything. I wasn't afraid.

Having said that, one thing I could see so vividly in my imagination was me standing in my laundry room, succumbing to the feelings of bitterness, borderline rage. I was going to expel these feelings at someone, anyone. I could see the anger and frustration bubbling up, but how to stop the emotional outburst that I knew was coming? If this could even happen when I am alone with my thoughts and my own imagination, imagine what damage I could wreak on the people who were supporting me. My mantra provided the right tool to deliver what I needed in a way that also validated to others my commitment to the work.

My mantra acts as a moment in time, one that brings me back to the here and now and one that reminds me what is actually meaningful in my world. Before that, I was not what you call a mantra kind of girl. In fact, you could say that I thought the whole idea was kooky.

To that end, I found a "witch doctor "– as I liked to call her – one of those nutty, kind of offbeat, non-traditional medicine masters, in the mountain village where we have a holiday home. It was dumb luck, I suppose. As many Swiss are into alternative medicines and as the village is not that big, it was not unlikely that we found each other. So, I made an appointment and, surprisingly, liked it. We began each session with a cup of tea and a chat. Talking about my stroke was not my favorite thing to do. However, the witch doctor insisted. We would then move to her therapy room where she focused on acupressure, unblocking my chakras, and massage.

She also insisted that I spend two hours, three times a week with her. While I found that a full-on commitment, I had faith in what she represented. You see, with all the therapeutic influences surrounding me, I could spend night and day working and still not even touch upon most of them. In order to make the most of my recovery, I throw myself into whatever I choose to do. The truth is that I am fully exposing myself and my deepest, darkest flaws to whomever is on the receiving end. Trust is paramount.

Could I put my recovery in her hands? I put myself out there, diligently working, 2 hours of precious time per day. After some weeks, while on the train from Klosters back to Zürich for my NOVA MRI, my left hand touched my right hand just on the point where my finger meets my nail bed. Amazingly, I could feel something. A slight sensation was just barely there. Of course, it could have been any of the exercises that I was doing, but it could have also been the "voodoo."

Cognitively, I grew significantly over those weeks. I had help from my new-found friends and fellow stroke survivors, Debbie and Wendy. I joined many stroke support groups, though I didn't find them particularly helpful. Instead, I found that personal introductions and those survivors that I met through Instagram were much more meaningful, as I prefer one-on-one relationships. A kind colleague of Johan's named Dawn put me in touch with Debbie. Debbie was a godsend. She made me feel like everything that I was feeling was normal. We talked about our experiences in a deep, honest, and non-judgmental manner that you only have when you've shared an experience with someone. I confided in her that I was losing weight and I was worried. Debbie told me to buy a Nutri-Bullet to drink my calories. I told her that when I go to take my daily nap, I meditate instead. Debbie told me that getting my sleep was more important in the early days. I cherished our new friendship.

A client-turned-friend put me in touch with Wendy sometime over the summer. She was just what the doctor ordered. She is spunky and kept me in stitches each time we spoke. She, through her fair share of health-related problems, had turned a shitty situation into a learning opportunity each time. It was no use to resist her enthusiasm. Her moxie was contagious. She had me hooked on trying new things to help my cognitive development, like Duo Lingo to learn another language, or puzzles, or Sudoku. Wendy also is a big believer in alternative methods of healing, like tapping and visualization.

Wendy spoke a language that I understood. Because she had survived the same kind of stroke as I just a few years earlier, there was an indelible bond between us. Her words were the antithesis of every doctor and almost every therapist that I'd spoken to. I tried everything that she suggested. While I gave up on tapping and Sudoku, I developed a strong belief in visualization and meditation. Wendy sent me links to meditate with Deepak Chopra and her "bible" as she called it from Dr. David Hamilton, an author who wrote about visualization healing the brain.

My summer was filled with amazing influences as I dug into Wendy's gifts. I learned from her "bible" that visualization can literally alter your body on a cellular level.

In other words, I could help my artery heal! I was driven to do anything to assist!

I was so excited that I couldn't contain myself. Over dinner, I explained my vision of the artery healing to my children and they also became excited. I wanted to involve them in the healing process. So I asked them to draw me pictures to match my vision. Each and every night, I closed my eyes and visualized tiny marshmallows padding my carotid artery wall with love. I introduced humor as well as my own personal touches, like swaddling my artery cells in almond milk or blueberries or whatever healthy food I ate that day.

*If you want to transform yourself through visualization, visit my website www.staciebroek.com. Click "Free Tools" in the main menu.*

I didn't realize that, since 20 February, I had been metaphorically holding my breath. Cautiously, I began to let myself breathe. I had made it this far, to the point where I recovered enough to drive a short distance and to create my very own treatment plan. I wasn't task-based in my thinking or concrete in my efforts anymore. I chose how I wanted to spend my time. I began to incorporate more daily life-based activities. The liberation was freeing.

Although I didn't see the pattern at the time, in retrospect, just when I think I can handle my therapies, my family, my life, that is precisely the time I bite off an unchewable piece.

By design and with my blessing, Johan left me and the children to go back to Tokyo for the summer. The responsibility of being the sole parent in residence was, at times, oppressive. There were days when I would have liked to stay in bed, watching Netflix and eating boatloads of Ben & Jerry's. There were times when I had to seriously pull myself up, give myself a talking to, and tell myself all of the reasons I had to fight.

# (al)ONE

When that didn't work, I fell down the rabbit hole of despair. For instance, take the ferret-of-a-man, the camp counselor, who was making my life, and that of my daughter's, utterly miserable while Johan was out of town. He allowed Lulu to be attacked verbally by a grown man, bullied her, failed to create a safe place for her, and lied about it to me. To top it all off, he then proceeded to send me threatening text messages.

My insides were screaming, "Hey, that deserves a slap in the face!" I felt small in comparison to the situation. I was still not myself, and I had no idea how to handle the problem. This was a man from the same town as us. My friends send their children with him skiing in the winter and to his summer tennis camp. He knew that I had suffered a stroke. How dare he? I was outraged.

On the other hand, I didn't trust my instincts. Every time he would text me or speak to my children, I second-guessed myself on how to deal with it. My stroke disabled my perception of right and wrong. It disallowed me to see the distinction between normal parenting, sticking up for your child in a proper way, and going haywire by punching someone in the face. My basic executive functions were severely compromised. Things like the ability to emotionally regulate myself were reduced to that of a toddler. Knowing this actually made it much harder for me to respond to the bullying.

I had visions of me going to the township and filing a complaint against him and visions of me in a punch up with him. What was right? I didn't know any more. At the end of the day, I took my father-in-law to meet with him. Even with my father-in-law, the most calm and collected man I know, we were unable to find a fitting solution. I felt that the camp counselor was a lying, cheating creep. I was worried that this instinct was a "stroke thing" but my father-in-law confirmed my judgment: the guy was a sleaze.

My brain had its work cut out for it, trying to come with a solution that was fitting. Through all of my work, the non-traditional methods like meditation and essential oils, coupled with the traditional therapeutic approaches, I gradually began to act more like an adolescent, and then more like a young adult. It was a slow process, but a definite improvement on the toddler-like impulses of my earlier recovery days.

Emotionally, I did the work. How I managed not to slap that man in the face (which I would have enjoyed just a few short months before) was a token of that work. I showed a level of emotional restraint which would definitely have been impossible in the first few months following my stroke.

What got me through to the other side was this thought: "I have three little ones to live for, and I'm determined to do just that." I was willing to try anything. I tried everything from the medical, to the non-traditional methods, to trying other kooky approaches. Because I had the power and the will.

My children saw their mother, this strong, fiery woman, reduced to an infant. I was broken. In time, I was attempting to become their mom again, but I was struggling to muddle through. I think the magic lies within us, as parents, to see the golden nugget of opportunity nestled in among the pain of our children. They have been rock stars, understanding me and my limitations from the get-go. But, how can I explain to them what I'm going through when I don't even understand it myself?

That golden nugget of opportunity – that's all we have to show our children. Instead of pretending to have it all figured out, we've tried to give them something greater.

Instead of finding a solution, as we're meant to do as adults, we've given them the authority to make real changes.

Along the way of revamping this new Stacie 2.0, many things have had to undergo reconstruction, including our family life, understanding the web of connections that we have built as expats, and our roles in both. Since I was my biggest cheerleader for home-based rehabilitation, it behooved me to make it work, not just for me, but for Johan and the children as well.

However, this was a lot of pressure to put on a marital relationship. We were suffering. Frankly we needed some time. Time without the children. Time without my therapies. Time to just be. Johan's parents offered to take the children for a couple nights and, gratefully, we took the opportunity to reconnect and just be alone.

I knew we could not neglect the reconstruction of our marriage. I was, on one hand, motivated by Johan's strength and capability to pull the weight, but on the other hand, I was at a loss of how I could ever recover quick enough to end the purgatory that he was in. There were cracks jutting out from our relationship, sharp edges which we had seen before but, in the spirit of day-to-day life, we just ignored. My stroke forced us to deal with every issue in a very real way. There was no escape. I was willing to work on our relationship, just as I was willing to work on all facets of my recovery, but I was in no way under the illusion that it could be accomplished in a few nights. But spending some time alone together at home seemed like a great start.

The thing about coming home after a tragedy, is that you need more than just a house, a building that you call yours. I found that coming home to Switzerland that summer left me in a weird place. It had stayed the same, with its grassy mountains and its late sunsets, but I had changed. I wasn't the Stacie I knew, or that everyone expected me to be. I had to find a new rhythm, to reconnect and rediscover what made this place home in the first place. I needed to find my heart and soul.

I was sitting in the garden, having my speech therapy with Seth, when two Bernese Mountain Dogs came bounding towards me. I couldn't stop smiling. They were just so happy. Just then, I heard their owner calling for them. Could it be? Those two dogs, shockingly, belonged to a friend of mine, Shona. I knew Shona from my event planning days in Zürich—but why was she in Klosters?

Seeing Shona there, out of place, amazed me in the best possible way. It turned out that she had bought a flat next door; the coincidence was eerie. For me, it was if she was put there right in my path, to embrace me and lift me up.

Over the course of the summer, going for long walks or sitting with wines in our garden, I believed that was exactly what Shona was doing. Through her infectious smile, her wicked sense of humor and gentle voice, she was just being herself but also exactly what I needed. Shona is the world's kindest human. She's the one who would stop everything to help. She was also the one who bridged the gap between me coming home and feeling as if I came home.

As we flew back to Tokyo at the end of the summer, I pondered the events of the past eight weeks. We had been home, in Switzerland, away from the hot and steamy concrete jungle that Tokyo turns into each year. All we'd had to do was get up, play tennis, walk in the mountains, and then enjoy a BBQ.

I turned to my children and asked them what they liked from their summer holiday. The answer was pretty genuine and simple. Like all kids, their summer meant unstructured time to play football and eat ice cream with more swimming and less of a schedule. They loved staying up late while playing tag with the neighborhood children. For children who have been through something traumatic, of course their truth is a little bit more complicated than this seemingly straightforward answer. Their truth is just a dream.

The summer with all of its firsts—the first time staying alone with the kids, the first time I was responsible for their meals, the first time going out of my medicinal comfort zone —was messy. Although there wasn't any tennis for me, I spent much of my time walking or simply sitting in the fresh mountain air, and enjoying the best BBQs, made with love by a mom and a wife who was getting better.

Like a bricklayer laying down stones, my recovery could only be built a single layer at a time. Before our lives were turned upside down, I was happily walking down the path of my life, blissfully unaware. My life was good. I was happy. It could have rolled on this way forever, as far as I was concerned. Then this, a stroke, and I suddenly find myself staring at this new Stacie 2.0 and I am not sure that I find mantras kooky anymore. In fact, I can imagine that the me that I'm striving towards is much more intuitive and wiser. There will be many changes in the way I relate to the world.

# CHAPTER 12
## Back to Reality
*Week 27 - 45: Hi, my name is Dan.*

Our return to Tokyo at the end of the summer brought with it a crash course in reality. We were fighting the return to schedules and to normalcy. However, at the end of the day, I think we all craved the routine that going to school afforded us.

I had a new bounce in my step. Not only was I eight weeks further along in my recovery–I returned to Tokyo stronger and more capable than I had been when I left–but something had changed in my emotional attitude, eliciting a powerful shift from within. My work over the summer had given me the foundation to consider what I really wanted. I had the power to decide which type of relationship I do or do not enjoy with myself. It didn't matter if the old Stacie was a mean hard-ass. The Stacie 2.0 could be made of marshmallows and candy floss. I had that power.

Fueled by our collective need for consistency, coupled with my newfound mindset, we rolled up to school on the first day. I was particularly eager to meet the new Head of School who was replacing Lorraine, a woman I considered a legend. I made a beeline towards him and he eagerly accepted me by holding out his hand, giving me the standard "Hello, my name is Dan."

It still embarrasses me to think about my cringe-worthy response. I was caught in mid-handshake and I just could not form the right words. I made a bunch of silly comments, all under my breath, just willing the name Stacie to come to me. Sadly, it did not. It was just sitting there, in the back of my brain, taunting me. That seemed like the longest handshake ever.

Suddenly, I knew it! I knew my name! As the words were coming out, I said proudly, "Good morning, I am Dan!" As soon as I said them, I realized they weren't the right words; I wanted to swallow them whole. So utterly awkward. So, I did what any woman in my situation would do. I acted supremely justified, as if I was totally in the right, because of course my name is Dan. And why are you staring at me like that? Are you waiting for something? I turned on my heel and scurried away, leaving Johan in the dust of my socially awkward moment.

In truth I was suffering on a day to day basis with getting my words out. Because I had been working two hours per day, each day, with Seth, my speech therapist, I was able to gain ground on my communication skills. My aphasia had improved so that I could sometimes form words with concentration and I had memorized a few simple sentences which could be used in everyday situations. But, I didn't want to be *that girl*. The girl who couldn't even introduce herself to another human being.

The girl who always comes up with the wrong word at the wrong time.

Sometimes we could find hilarity in the situations, for instance, the time I offered my son a fossil for dinner. I meant a chicken wing. Or the time that I was walking through Tokyo's crowded streets and turned to Lulu, scaring the daylights out of her, and asked, "Is that guy still following us?" I meant Friso. (He was, for the record.) Or the time I was sitting at Starbucks with Cleo, when our attention was grabbed by two friendly dogs at the table next to us. We enjoyed their company and, when they were leaving, Cleo asked me which of the two was my favorite. I promptly answered her with, "The green dog." I meant the white dog.

On a subconscious level my brain was frantically searching in my dictionary to complete the idea that I liked the white dog. But it seemed to have become impatient; it just took the first thought it found and ran with it, which left me standing here, liking the supposed green dog or renaming myself Dan.

A few weeks later, I had my leg taped by my physiotherapist to correct my chronic Babinski reflex and, consequently, to retrain my brain. Walking with my foot in a permanent spastic ball was affecting my entire right side, from my calf to my neck. Everything hurt. A Babinski reflex means that, upon receiving stimulus, your big toe goes up and the others fan out. This reflex is a perfectly normal response to stimuli in babies or toddlers, but if it happens to anyone older than two years old, it can indicate that a lurking nervous system disorder is affecting you. In my case, it was a symptom of my stroke and my big toe was stuck in the permanent position of going up. The idea was that if the tape could make my toes go in the right direction, it would help to re-jig the neurons that this was the normal position and simmer my reflex down.

I was willing to try anything and I'd read that taping could help. I wasn't at all self-conscious about the neon orange tape running up my leg. As far as I was concerned, it was a simple step in my recovery. The thing is that I wasn't really ready for the comments that my friends would make. When I went to pick the children up from school, everyone kept asking, "Did you do something to your foot?" I had to stop myself from the shouty response, "Of course I did. I had a stroke!" because that's not considered polite.

At home, my mistakes were amusing, if sometimes frustrating. However, in social situations, I found myself less comfortable and I was less likely to laugh at my speech faux pas. I, inevitably, would try to cover up what I meant with nonsensical chatter or blurt out that I had a stroke, leaving my partner in conversation knocked for six.

The thing is I was feeling more comfortable in my skin, which caused me to take more chances; but the more chances I took, the more likely that I would stick my foot in my mouth. Like the time that I was speaking to someone who asked me how long I'd lived in Switzerland. Instead of answering his very straightforward question, what he got was me twisting around myself in apologies. My ability to do the simplest of maths has all but vanished. *I can do this* was all I kept thinking. I knew that we had arrived there in 2005 and we left in 2017. Simple, right? Not for me. I was gobsmacked at my inability to do what should have been an effortless calculation.

I wasn't familiar with the term "invisible disability" until that point. It didn't make sense. I was walking amongst my peers, my family and my friends trying to fit in with the banter, with the fast-paced rhythm. Inside, I had to work a bit harder to keep my grounding, if I could at all. I had to work on my disability first, so I might have seemed a bit slow, or a bit on-the-back-foot or just plain not myself anymore. I looked like the same old Stacie, perhaps even better. Inside, however, I was still suffering the lasting physical, emotional, and cognitive effects of surviving a stroke. Had I been in a wheelchair, my arm in a cast, or simply had bright orange tape running up my leg, everyone would see what I needed. Because my disability was not visible to the naked eye, I found it exhausting and troublesome in the most complicated way to figure out.

I couldn't simply react to emergencies because my whole life at this time was one big emergency. After suffering her fifteenth bout of tonsillitis in eighteen months, Lulu was getting her tonsils out. I'd finally managed to find our way through the medical hierarchy to a doctor who could perform a tonsillectomy on her. It was akin to finding a needle in a haystack.

Had we been at home in Switzerland, we would simply have gone to our pediatrician and he would have recommended an Ear, Nose & Throat specialist who, in turn, would have recommended a tonsillectomy. In Japan, our medical care was more ad hoc. There was a children's doctor that all of the expats went to, but I didn't trust him. So we were left to our own devices, which I imagine would have been much easier without a stroke clouding everything. Yet with extreme care and difficulty, I managed.

So putting on our brave faces, we arrived at the same hospital that I had lived in for six weeks, this time for Lulu's operation. There was something uncanny about going back to the hospital where I experienced the single most debilitating, horrifying and crippling event I have experienced in my life. Weirdly, it also felt secure, like we could make it through. We checked in for the five days we were told the operation needed. I had no idea why it would take this long. But, as good patients, we didn't ask questions.

I tremble with fear each time I replay Lulu going under anesthesia. As her mother, I was allowed to watch. There was something about watching her, my courageous, slender too-young-to-die angel walking up to the operating table, climbing onto it and breathing in the gas. It was too much to bear. I wailed in shock. I had to be escorted out.

The waiting was unbearable for Lulu to come out of surgery. I was snappy and bit off Johan's head more than once. Katja was there to keep me calm, but she apparently thought that I was in the wrong and she scolded me more than once. *How dare she!* I kept thinking.

I stayed in the hospital with Lulu that night; the day after her tonsils were removed, I quickly scurried home to say good morning to Friso and Cleo before they caught the bus. I was greeted with another emergency. I recalled before taking Lulu to the hospital that Cleo had been complaining that her pierced earring was bothering her for a couple days. As I couldn't deal with it at the time, I'd let it go. That morning when I returned to the house, she came to me with the biggest, pussiest, most definitely infected ear that I ever saw. "Oh shit!" was all that came to my mind. It was like the earlobe swallowed the earring. It had sandwiched the earring from the front.

I tried to take the back off to get the stupid earring out, but with my right hand still incapable of feeling, I couldn't do it. I shouted for Johan, who, bless him, made a bad situation worse. As he was looking at it, I guess he thought that with brute force he would get it out. So, he pushed it back, the wrong way, towards her head. She screeched in pain. The little stone of the earring was now pushed back, the wrong way, into her ear.

There we sat. I had no idea what the hell to do. I had one kid waiting for me in the hospital and another one to be admitted? I couldn't think. It was just too much. All I wanted to do was curl up under my duvet and hide until the world disappeared. I couldn't take Cleo to the Emergency Room because, even in English, I couldn't find the words right now. How would I explain to a Japanese nurse what had happened? So, I sent Friso with the school bus and packed Squidge in the car to go to the only English-speaking doctors' office in Tokyo. I called them on the way to notify them that we, a crazy mother and her mangled child, were on our way.

It was like being in a *Bad Moms* movie that you never want to star in. I burst into the practice like I was on fire, insisting that Squidge be properly taken care of. My damaged brain was on overload. I couldn't piece the puzzle together. My mind kept buzzing from one of my precious daughters to the other, both of whom were hurting. I couldn't stand it.

The first doctor was nice enough, but his suggestion was to take her to the emergency room. I not-so-silently insisted that they take care of her here and now. We were made to sit for the longest time in the waiting room. However I couldn't sit. I needed to do something. The frantic thoughts wouldn't leave my mind alone. This never-ending cycle, this perseverating on one thing only, is a symptom of my brain damage. I get stuck in the well of "what ifs" and I cannot climb out.

I was about to climb out of my skin. Just then, we were called into another doctor's office, who thankfully took charge of the situation. He deftly laid her down, numbed her ear, efficiently extracted the earring, and bandaged it up.

When it was all over, I could feel resentment creeping inside of every cell of my being. I was mad. At Johan. I couldn't believe that he was the cause of my little angel's suffering. What was going on with him? Was he so up his own arse? Couldn't he have known, if he studied Cleo's ear for just a millisecond, that he was pushing it the wrong way? I tried to give him the benefit of doubt, but he just seemed so far away. I couldn't capture him. So, the gap between us grew even larger. I had a feeling that we were going to fall into it, if we weren't careful.

More crises came with the holidays. Thanksgiving dinner came around and everyone was excited. I made tacos with all the fixins instead of my usual turkey dinner and invited Katja's family. Afterwards, as I was cleaning up, Johan left to go meet a client for drinks on his bicycle. I found him on the couch in the morning with dried-up blood on his head and face, coming down his arms. Apparently, he had crashed his bike. I immediately ushered him to our bathroom before the children could catch a glimpse, told him to clean himself up and take a taxi to the medical center. We spent the remainder of the afternoon at the same hospital I'd been in, with the same neurologists I'd had, going over scans of Johan's head. I was livid.

In an effort to gain a semblance of control, I started canceling everything that we had planned to do. Dinner plans with friends. Our family trip to Kyoto, to celebrate our fifteen-year anniversary. A sayonara cheese fondue party. In hindsight, I know that it was wrong to pull the plug on all these events, but I didn't see how I could behave naturally in front of our children or our friends. I couldn't fake it. I was beside myself in outrage. Silently, I also knew that if anything would drive Johan crazy, it would be that. I was needling him.

I found it exhausting, after a summer of growth and strength, to return to this place of uncertainty. I felt as though my friends, for instance, had moved on and were past caring about me and for me. I felt that, in their minds, my stroke had taken enough time from them. So it was up to me to step it up. I began masking my true identity because it didn't feel comfortable, didn't fit in with all of the expectations and speed that came with my life. Of course it was ridiculous to think like this, but I wanted and needed them to see me as their equal.

More and more I felt like a phony. I was caught in between wanting to make a full recovery and working my ass off to realize it, and pretending that I was recovered. My relationships were bearing the brunt of my anxieties. There was nothing that I wouldn't do to save them, but to shatter the illusion that made me feel comfortable wasn't easy. So, I continued to wear the mask of the old Stacie, because it made me feel better.

I was hiding myself, even from Johan. You say when you are married "until death do us part" and "in sickness and in health," but when push comes to shove, how you deal with your life-partner in times of crisis is simply foreign. The fact is that illness or a sudden life-changing-event causes turmoil, even wreaks havoc, on marital relationships.

I was no longer an equal. I had been placed like an infant, by something much larger and more forceful than me, in my husband's care. Something more urgent took over. Now, my husband was in charge. And I was not.

With time, the shift felt more natural, or maybe I had just succumbed to it. In any event, I couldn't get a break. He was a happy-go-lucky kind of guy. He enjoyed life to the fullest. Until this. This amount of responsibility—he not only had me to look after, care for and make decisions for, but also our children—was oppressive. I can only imagine that, in his mind, he was thinking that the whole kit and kaboodle was perched on his shoulders. Because it was.

Emotions are amplified when you are facing this amount of stress with your spouse. Things flew off the tips of our tongues much more fluidly than before. We ran into potentially disastrous situations and before we knew it, we were knee-deep in this thing, this vicious circle that encapsulated both of us. We were falling victim to a whirlwind of emotions, none of which we could fathom, doing nothing to stop the downward spiral. The fact is, we both thought we were right, and self-righteous indignation took over.

They don't teach this in physiotherapy, or in speech therapy or handbooks to recover from your stroke. This massive emotional stress took over our lives and we both thought we were right. He was going out, coming home late, and not pulling his weight with the children. I retaliated by canceling dinner parties and trips to see the sites of Japan. I was cold and disapproving, focused only on me; I was not fun to be around. He retaliated by shutting down his emotions.

In the beginning, from my slanted, concrete, black-and-white view of the situation, I could not help but judge him. I shouted inside my mind that it was I who suffered a stroke. Jesus! What was wrong with him? I am sure that if he could have, Johan would have loved to take a trip, just so he could feel anything but the immense burden of his life. Since the moment Johan found me mid-stroke, everything from making decisions when I was on the operating table, to handling the incomprehensible Japanese bills, to our harrowing lives today, his life has taken an unwanted about-face.

Just the same, I would love to wake up, just once, and not have to deal with my very stupid speech impediments or my inability to calculate simple math. The thing is, there are no in-betweens. The alternative to both of the situations is hopeless.

There were days when we both wanted to slam the front door and just keep walking, to throw in the towel on us and our marriage. My stroke caused a huge disruption in our lives, one that I still only hope we can recover from. It's like tiptoeing through a battlefield, where every step is just laced with the potential to hit a landmine. Except that we were running carelessly. And dangerously.

To those people who knew about my stroke, it left me feeling a bit dispirited. I was caught in between, knowing that no one is eating and breathing my stroke, and an impossible feeling of being punished. Surely people have a bit of sensitivity? Or don't people know what suffering a stroke entails?

I felt very sorry for those unsuspecting people who fell down the rabbit hole with me, people who didn't know about my stroke and, perhaps, wanted to keep it that way. When those folks asked, "Did you do something to your foot?" I was at a loss. Of course, there was an easy, simple, uncomplicated way to answer, but I either couldn't find the words or I rebelled against them. The naked truth of it was that I didn't feel the need to make excuses for my deficiencies.

I am not ashamed of my stroke. But, what do you do when something strikes that's more powerful than you, something that's too heavy to grasp on your own? How the hell do you put one foot in front of the other? How do you go on, when your entire body has failed you? Wouldn't it keep you lying awake at night, or at the very least, keep you from living your life with spontaneity?

These were things that were playing over and over in my brain, things that ripped me to the core of my being. It left me wondering, how do I build that trust once more? Is it at all possible without making significant changes?

Thanks to all of the work I did on myself over the summer, I felt discouraged and beaten-down, but not incapable. Although I didn't identify it as such at the time, I continued the work on my emotional recovery. I kept on diving into the deepest end of the pool, sometimes forgetting my water wings. I kept on believing that the path was right, even though it was foggy and dark and unknown.

Visualization, meditation, and deep breathing all were significant medicines to heal my soul and, in turn, my body. They acted as balm to my otherwise chafed brain and I found solace in them. Visualizing that my carotid artery would heal itself became almost urgent. I needed to believe that I could play a part in the healing process.

I remembered something that my mother told me: that if I believe in something with my whole heart, then it's true. Take Santa Claus, for instance. I remember asking her whether or not he existed. Her reply? "Do you believe?" As a child, I didn't question how the gifts appeared every Christmas morning. What mattered is that they were there, that I believed that they would be.

I figured that the same could be said about recovery. I've talked to a lot of people, some far-out-there and some closer to earth. They all agree that while research on the brain has come leaps and bounds, nobody really knows what we are capable of. It's all about the work that we put in. My recovery is not just physical. It's cognitive. It's verbal. And it's emotional. To fully recover, it will take me years, and that's only if I continue to do the work.

When I started along this journey, a difficult path that I didn't want to go on, two things became abundantly clear. The first is that it is all up to me if I crash and burn, or make a decent start on my recovery. I'm responsible. No one else. The thing is, no one actually understands what I am going through. So how could anyone else but me help me? In itself, this is positively freeing. It's like a small get-out-of-jail-free card and to never feel guilty about it.

The second is I am a fighter. I didn't want to just recover from this stroke, I wanted to *kick its ass*. That feeling is a very powerful one. I wanted to scream it from the mountain tops.

I finally had to admit to that unsuspecting man, who was just making conversation about how long I lived in Switzerland, that I had had a stroke. In polite societies, we've been conditioned to avoid certain subjects. My stroke, although it causes me not an ounce of embarrassment, falls into this category. So that easy, simple, uncomplicated way to answer rolls, rather distastefully, into honesty. I was not following the rules. I was revealing much too much. And I didn't care.

So there I sat in this dichotomous situation. On one hand, hoping that my friends and family accept me just the way that I am. I wanted them to note my vulnerabilities and to care about them. On the other hand, I was working my ass off to cover up my deficiencies. I suspected that I couldn't have it both ways. It was putting my friends, family or people I met on the street, in an impossible position. I wanted everyone to see my best side.

Even I was falling prey to my own criticisms. Why does he walk so slowly? What's wrong with him? I slowly began to notice the double-edged-sword-ness of it all. I was playing king, a ruler with no perception of what her supporters were going through.

# (al)ONE

When I was living in New York, it was baffling to me why anyone would live in a country where they couldn't speak the language. Then I moved to Japan. I was also living in a country without speaking any Japanese. The realities of living in another culture, the manifold reasons that bring us to lands far from our own - family, career, and other - all of these were invisible to me before I experienced them.

The veneer that everyone sees is just a facade, the put-together Stacie. What's happening behind the scenes is me clawing like mad to cover up my strokey behaviors. That's the feisty in me. I realized that I am a pit bull. My stroke dared to cross my path.

This situation has forced me to come out of the privileged, almost jaded position I was in in life. It's forced its will on me. It's taught me that I have to get up each and every day, fight with integrity, and hope that I see progress. It's a long-term war. Sometimes I win a battle. Other times, I am like a polished, confident woman acting strangely, saying weird things or switching off, showing a momentary crack in my mask.

# CHAPTER 13
## Regrets and Realities
*Weeks 46 - 52: I am a bitch and a bully.*

I had assembled, very carefully, every bit of the knowledge that I had gained since my stroke. I believed that with this process I was growing into a kinder, more thoughtful and stronger human. All the same, my stroke brought me down to my most basic, decidedly primitive, instincts. I was a pit bull, clawing like hell against the uphill battle of recovery. My deficits were still there but I felt that I was getting closer to my 2.0.

The days ran into each other, filled with therapies and mixed with the normalities of everyday life. We spent the Christmas holidays with the children in New Zealand. I don't know why, but it was filled with stops and starts, as if we weren't sure where to begin. I fought with Johan a lot–in front of the children, when we were alone, and in front of anyone who dared cross my path. I was mad at him.

I was out for a run one day when my sister, Nikki, rang my mobile. I let the call go to voicemail. I knew that I should not pick up the phone when I saw her number appear. I knew that if I did, it would not go well. I was not in the right mindset.

We are three years apart in age. Just enough to have very different memories of our childhood, but as adults, to secure a solid relationship. If we worked on it. She married her high school sweetheart, moved across the street from her in-laws and in the same town as our parents. While I was living in a rented NYC shoebox apartment, not knowing how I was going to make my rent, she was building her dream home and planning her first baby. We were both happy with our different choices.

We could read each other's minds. It was eerie. We were always on the same wavelength. I can remember to this day how we rocked the family Cranium game. It was down to us: if we won this point, we'd win the whole game. It was my turn to act out the prompt from the secret pad. I held my breath, closed the pad and got down on the floor. The tension built. I acted my heart out, driving a pretend race car, making sound effects as I slipped the gears higher and higher and screeched around the corners of a pretend racetrack. Nikki in two seconds flat shouted the correct answer. *Low rider.* I will never forget the love and the bond that we share and, for me, it was most apparent that day with our loved ones. I love her with all of my heart.

But, on this particular day, I knew that I shouldn't take her call. I hadn't prepared for this phone call, as I had for the previous time we had spoken, months before. That time, I'd had a script planned out so she could not surprise me. I had covered all the bases.

The truth is that our relationship had been rather unstable over the past six months. Perhaps it started long before but we both knew how to deal with it. My sister, despite our connection, had hurt me immensely many times over the past years, and a great deal since my stroke. Although I didn't see it at the time, I always felt guilty for my life choices around her and she had an uncanny ability to make me feel punished for them. For example, I'll never forget the time that she told me in a matter-of-fact, off-the-cuff manner, while driving down the motorway, that I had been replaced as her first born's godmother because I moved to Europe. Because of my choice to leave the country, I had been dismissed.

There were many such examples. Many telephone conversations from abroad ended with "When are you guys going to come home?" and each visit that we made home, she made needling remarks about my parenting style. Culturally, she wanted me to fit into her Pennsylvanian life, and it was great each time we made the long trip there, but she never really seemed interested in *my* life.

We both ignored our differences. Me because I didn't have a choice. If I wanted a relationship with my sister, this is what I had to do. And Nikki, because, in her mind, she thought that she was doing the right thing.

I could handle these conflicts because I knew in my heart that she loved me and would always be there when I needed her. I thought that I didn't have to question that. When I suffered my stroke, she couldn't be there with me. I understood her dilemma. She is a school teacher and I was in Japan. I always thought that the onus laid solely on me. Nikki is not as obsessed with travel and other cultures as I am. Nikki has a full life in Pennsylvania. I believed that, in some small way, that gave her an excuse. I had to travel if I wanted to see my sister and her family. Physically, Nikki was off the hook.

What I did expect from her, in those darkest months of my life, was for her to be there emotionally, not just for me but for Johan and the children as well. I expected her to be a support system from afar. I expected her to lend an ear to my kids, whose mother was struggling for her life. I would expect her to let Johan know that she was just a phone call away if he needed someone to scream at, to joke with, or just listen. I expected her to grant me and my family the simple gift of tolerance.

In the weeks immediately following my stroke, I couldn't handle FaceTime calls or open-ended text messages asking about my status. Although my mother and Johan explained this to Nikki many times, she didn't let up. I can only imagine when someone you are connected to on the other side of the world is facing a life-or-death situation you want like hell to be there. However, I also think that if you can't be there, it is incumbent upon you to do the right thing.

She reached out to the children in dribs and drabs. In fact, Cleo's birthday was just a week after my stroke and all my daughter received from my sister was a simple text message. I think the biggest offense was when Nikki made an inappropriate, foolish offer to Johan that the children could fly to America for the summer to be with her. I needed my children and they needed me. It was an ignorant and self-centered, if charitable, attempt to be helpful.

My sister was clinging to me, but not in ways that were good for me at that time, and it started a grim downwards cycle. My inability to control my emotions and my disjointed communication skills meant that each time we spoke, it was a potential disaster. We communicated less and less over the months. I found it heartbreaking. I needed my sister. It angered me that she wasn't there emotionally. I pleaded, with my tangled-up communication skills, for her to be there in my life, in a way that I could handle. No text messages that require a response on my part! Communications that update me on her life, little anecdotes or jokes. Anything uplifting! Alas, it all hinged on the phone call that I was about to have.

Surviving the stroke meant that I could no longer hold anything back. If I didn't prepare in advance for tricky conversations my concrete thinking would block me, and if I got flustered, I could easily be provoked. So, I let voicemail kick-in the first time. And the second time. The third time, however, I got worried that something was wrong back in Pennsylvania. So I accepted her call. It was like a car crash. We fell into the same old verbal routine, her with her superior, calm voice and me with my needy whine, cackling like a crow.

I knew that the words were coming more quickly than I could process them. I knew that I should stop! However, my damaged brain couldn't stop the well of emotions from spouting out. So, I let her have it. All of it. Without holding back. All of the hurt, the anger, came raging out. The words were spewing out faster than I could possibly catch them. They were all true, but did they need to be said?

"You never reach out to me!!!" I cried.

"Well, you never do either," she stated calmly.

"I went to Switzerland to have a second opinion! It was a big deal! And you never asked anything about it! You didn't even ask how the kids are handling it!" I screeched.

"Well, did you call and ask anything about me or my family?" came the infuriating reply.

"Do you know anyone who's ever had a stroke?" I thought that if we explored this topic together, then perhaps it would level the playing field. In my head, this could be the starting point of understanding.

To my surprise, she replied, "Yes, several."

To her credit, she tried to placate me, but I had heard it all before. Her cavalier protest over the last few months was always, "Yes, I agree with you that I could have kept in better touch, but I am here now. It's up to you. If we don't start somewhere, then we're nowhere." Until this day, two days before Christmas, I hadn't heard from her in over three months, since our birthdays in September. She was trying to appease me with her same ole same ole. And today I wasn't buying it. On this day, I found her galling and up her own ass.

So, I didn't back down. Eventually, she said, "You are a bitch and a bully!" and slammed the phone down. I was ashamed and very angry. As I went back to the house, her words were echoing in my ears. They shook me all the way to my core.

I didn't know how to focus on mundane things like preparing for Christmas, my absolute favorite holiday, when my world had been shattered like this. Nikki didn't just hang up the phone that day, she cut off all communication with me and my family. By the time I had sat down in the evening, she had quit my mailing list, where I send weekly updates about my recovery; unfollowed me and the children on social media; and blocked us on her accounts. I was taken aback, and an overwhelming sense of loss and despair crept over me.

In the days following those leading up to the most joyous holiday ever, I retreated. I went inwards. I questioned everything about myself, my relationships, and everything I was doing. It was the first time since surviving the stroke that I found myself in such a profound crisis of faith. It was brutal.

Was I in the wrong? Was it her? Was she right? Does it even matter? I felt the loss, significantly. I experienced a wide range of emotions, but despite the guilt and sorrow, anger was first and foremost in my heart. It encapsulated my being. I had suffered a stroke! How could she talk to me in such a way?! Had she no compassion?

I pushed my sister and every detail of that conversation away, tucked deep inside my mind. The pain was so intense, I didn't feel ready to deal with any of it. There was so much to focus on already.

Just as I thought when dealing with my marriage, you have doctors and therapists to help you physically recover, but I have often wondered who helps your soul recover from its loss? How do you go about the process of mending those broken pieces of the puzzle, those that, perhaps, needed fixing even before the crisis?

I went into mourning for my pre-stroke life, where everyone knew where they stood, even if it was wrong. For instance, before my stroke, I never sent birthday cards or presents. Everyone joked (at least I did—perhaps I was the only one) that they all got lost in the post. That was okay for me then, but on this side of survival, I despised myself. It's not right! It certainly doesn't fit my concept of the new me. I am a perfectionist. No one is able to see me sweat. Why? So I am left with these weird aspects of my recovery. Ones that I never, in a million years, thought were wrong.

There is no magic formula. I am finding that with all aspects of my recovery, if I don't do the work, I cannot expect results. I've learned that asking questions about the relationships that matter to me is a good place to start. Can I make it right again? Do I even want to? How do I pick up the pieces of something that went so horribly wrong and mend them? What does it mean to have this person in my life, or not?

I found searching for answers to those extraneous questions cathartic, like having a one-way conversation with your soul. I spent months mulling those questions over and over in my mind. I made mental notes here and there, and watched with a certain amount of fascination as my brain formulated its answers. I thought to myself, *it will be done when I feel that I have fully explored all of my questions and found reasonable resolutions.* I found this truth-serum for the soul needed to brew and simmer until the perfect solution was concocted.

My husband has an unbelievable amount of zest for life and for living each day to its fullest. I want to model and bottle that enthusiasm! Can we get back to where we were last year? How? Do I want to reconstruct the relationship as it was? How? His bicycle accident on Thanksgiving and the way that I dealt with it, his retreating backwards into himself, act as proof that we have a long road ahead of us. The truth is, I have no idea what my stroke did, or does, to him. I am too busy fighting my own battles to understand his. What I know is that I love him with all of my being. So I keep that pot on the burner.

With my brain injury, I learned that to consider a multitude of options for a single situation; to have choices was better. It's too easy to fly by the seat of damaged pants, too easy to hurt those that you love. I found it crucial to give myself space to think outside the box.

In order to grow, I needed to readjust to my new normal, one where I cannot trust the first reactions of my brain and heart and, instead, give myself time. Finding the answers is not preventative in these situations, but it does help my soul find the peace that it so covets, if I remember them. Perhaps I had a damaged relationship with my sister before my stroke. Or perhaps I was the culprit. Either way, I found going through this process was remarkably cleansing.

It struck me that I am in charge of the process. Neither Johan, nor the children nor my friends can do this for me.

That thought propelled me to think deeply about my relationships and to accept them, warts and all. I realized I was frantically trying to make a connection between how others were acting and reacting to me and planning my next steps in succession, instead of accepting their behavior. The truth is, how I reacted to them was in my control all along.

I think back to the time as a child when I asked my mother about Santa Claus. I picture myself, dressed in my old flowered nighty, and my mother putting on her makeup, her long, glossy black hair cascading down her back. It seemed a question of faith that I asked her, "Is Santa real?" But her answer asked me to take control. I wanted to believe, so I did. I chose right then and there to believe. Likewise, I wasn't angry about the terrible things I said to my sister, but I was angry that I had said them. I didn't have the ability to take control.

Anger breeds resentment, which breeds more resentment. Before you know it, you are swimming in an angry pool of your own making. I don't blame myself, but looking back, I realize that I could have dealt with every heated situation differently. My last job in New York was on a team with what can only be described as a dictator of a director. As we were all in charge of our businesses, making money for the company, it behooved the owners to figure it out. So, a coach was brought in to work with us in a group setting.

I'll always remember what the coach said to us. "You can't control other people, but you have control over your reaction." She continued to say that if you don't like the situation, then change it. For me, this was like a breath of fresh air, an *aha* moment. Of course I couldn't change my boss, but I sure as hell could shift the impact they had on me. It was as if someone had sat me down and very harshly told me that I was placing blame unfairly.

Thankfully, I quit that job when I moved to London, but the coach's advice stuck with me, and I often can be heard telling my children the same thing. "You cannot control other people. You can only control your reaction." It's not always easy to do, and more complicated with a brain injury, to stop yourself and the rage from bubbling to the surface. However, I've taken these words to heart.

By reacting in such a malicious manner to that phone call, there were only losers. Nikki hung up on me and cut all ties to me and my family. I didn't want that. I would have liked her to be normal and have normal reactions! She couldn't have wanted that either. I would like to think that I was important to her, as well.

What changed when I had my major life-altering event is that I felt everything so utterly deeply. I realized that I couldn't keep insisting everyone played by my rules. I realized that instead of creating an image that I expect my friends or my family to be and all that they have to live up to, I recognized that I needed to form a more healthy habit of acceptance. It was as if lightning struck!

I think back to the time when we were all waiting for Lulu to come out of surgery and how pissed I felt at Katja. She kept chiding me about laying off Johan. I thought I had every right to be pissed at her. But the truth is, had she acted in any other way, she would not be the woman that I loved with my whole heart. Something much stronger than my emotions drew me towards her. The ripple in the pool of my life had brought me closer to kindness and acceptance, even though that is a heavy concept for someone in this stage of stroke recovery.

For me, there was a pleasant stage of ignorance when I didn't know how "broken" I was. I still remember thinking that I would be able to take my children away on their spring break and the crushing realization that I could not.

What followed was a massive struggle to fully come to grips with my deficits. And when I managed to do so, it hit me hard. I will always remember asking my doctors two things from my hospital bed. The first was, "Can I still travel to Switzerland this summer?" and the second was, "How long until I get back to normal?"

I did travel to Switzerland that summer, but I had to realize that "normal" is just *not a thing*. I asked that same question to my doctors, my therapists—hell, I even asked other stroke survivors. Depending on their level of competence and truth, I received a wide range of answers. I eventually realized that only I can decide what recovery looks like for me. No one else. Not my doctor. Not my mom. Not my therapist. Only I have that power.

Maria was one of wisest people I ever had the pleasure of knowing. Her wisdom led her down the path of peace with the healing process and the awareness to let that process spill over into other areas of her life. She was always searching for new drugs, new methods to heal her. She accepted herself fully, for better or for worse. She didn't take shit from anyone. In fact, she wrote her own rules for the life she wanted to lead.

Through my struggles and the sadness of my broken relationship with Nikki, I desperately wanted to believe that I was a force in my own life. Just like Maria, Katja and even my estranged sister, I wanted to imagine I had power over myself and my recovery. I started living out my own interpretations of what recovery meant to me. This was a huge step for me. Even now, it doesn't seem possible. How did I, always super-critical, always focused on achieving, make this pivot?

I managed because my stroke knocked me all the way down, to a deep, dark, scary place, without my faculties; there was no other choice. I was experiencing an intrinsic shift. I had to grab onto anything, everything that felt right and, in turn, leave the things that felt false. If I had been in a country where it was slightly more "normal," or at least not so foreign, I would have relied on the "experts" to guide me. The alley cat in me fought and clawed onto anything that I could imagine to help.

What I found was that there are no intrinsic limits placed on me or my recovery. I heard my doctors, the neurosurgeons who saved my life, telling me that I should not expect much more development after six months. After being initially scared to death, my thoughts changed to "To hell with that! I will be the only one who says it's enough!" To the doctor who said "You can talk. You can walk. You should be happy with it," to him, I screamed in my head "How the hell do you get off saying these brainless things to a survivor?" I might have mentally slapped him, as well.

But, when is it enough?

That led me to a place where I questioned everything about my recovery. On good days, I found it okay to not know what I was working towards, because, in my mind, it was all-embracing. I was in a place where virtually anything would propel me forward. However, darker days were spent mocking myself and thinking unkind thoughts. I'd already passed the six-month marker and my progress was no longer as apparent as it had been in the first six months. I would spend these darker days beating myself up with thoughts such as, "Why do I take speech therapy every day? It's not as if my speech is getting any better!" And so it went.

On those grim days, I tried to channel Kara, one of the most considerate humans I know. She never forgets a birthday, cards and presents shipped all over the world, sending thoughtful messages of hope exactly when I need them. Her instincts always let her know what to do when! On these days, I picture her telling me to take a beat. Slow down. It's okay. That I work so hard, it's more than enough! It's okay to not know where you're going. In fact, that's part of the joy! And then my sweet Kara wraps her arms around me in solidarity.

Once I was talking with a fellow stroke survivor about the way that others classify us. The way that doctors classify us. The way that we classify ourselves and the huge disparities in between. You see, what's on the outside doesn't necessarily match what's on the inside or what we perceive as our own deficiencies. We undeniably fall under the stigma that we are broken until we are better. That leaves me wondering: what is the definition of "better?"

The simple definition of recovery is restoring your mind and body. By this definition, I am unequivocally *not* better. Who gets to choose our version of better? Is it enough to be able to cook our own meals? To walk? To be able to make our own decisions? To be able to keep up with the fast pace of life?

Today I need so much more than my pre-stroke self did. I need you to stay by my side when we are in a new situation. I need you to treat me kindly, in a way that I didn't expect or require before. I need you to have patience with me.

I found this change, and the realization of it, an incredibly debilitating aspect of my stroke. I was full of independence before, but now I wait in the shadows to peek my head out and see if it's safe to enter your world. All hell breaks loose when I get it wrong, as I often do. I realized that most people don't see that side of me. They classify me as better, and that's unfair.

I have become a master of the black and white. There are no in-betweens for me. You either see a well-put-together master of disguise or a shockingly unraveled woman coming apart at the seams. In the words of a not-so-wise doctor: *You can walk. You can talk. You should be happy.*

I think by saying that, he made an erroneous, flawed judgement based on his perception of what "better" looks like. His cavalier, off-the-cuff remark made a lasting impression on me. I was mad. At him and at everyone who thinks that they have any right to make snap judgments on my recovery. As I paid the bill from that doctor's visit, I had to laugh. He classified me as broken, and that's also not fair.

It leaves me pondering the question, why do others have a say? For me, it is not enough to walk and talk again. I want to be able to create things. I want to run a marathon. I want to help my children with their maths homework. And if I decide along the way that better takes a different form, I want to have the ability to change my path. I want to figure out what Stacie 2.0 looks like through searching high and low, discovering what makes her tick and combing through all of her guts and glory.

Why does it matter to me? Shouldn't I just "get on with it?" With my recovery, with my life and everything in between? Who cares if you finish my sentences for me? Do I really mind if, from your perception, hobbling around on my good leg is "good enough?" Here's the thing: it *does* matter to me, and I would be lying if I said otherwise. I only want to surround myself with people who get it.

I am in the process of assembling an arsenal of therapists, doctors and a village of people who not only get it, but want for me to go through this process of redefining myself and come out better from it—my definition of better.

I can see how easy it is to give up. It just becomes too much and the expectations of us are either too low or too high. There are days when I seriously question myself. Do I have to go running or to physiotherapy or to speech therapy? I calculated how many hours I've spent in therapies during the first year since my stroke. It was over a whopping one thousand hours! That was precious time that could have been spent with my family, with my camera touring around Tokyo, or writing.

Emotionally, I will not fully recover unless I embrace what it means to me and champion the love and the change that it represents. It deserves a special place in my heart, one which I will always remember and respect. It also encapsulates my life's starting point, so to speak. It is as though everything has been brought suddenly to life and each year I'm celebrating my birthday. I've had to relearn, just as a baby. Along the steep road to my rebirth I feel I've gained, in a fundamental manner.

I've discovered that my sense of serenity and wellbeing is a part of me that I should not take for granted. I thought it was just an added bonus to meditate or to take thirty minutes to cleanse my face or to light a scented candle each time I was writing. As it turns out, these "bonuses" are all essential to my healing.

I've learned that I have to extend kindness to myself and others from the onset. I was always a hardcore woman with no time to take shit from anyone. It turns out that my stroke had other plans. It slowed me down and taught me the discipline of thoughtful behaviors. I've ascertained that not everyone can advocate for themselves. Learning this lesson makes me angry. I just want to stomp my feet in aggravation and lend them a voice.

I've figured out that mantras are not kooky.

My attitude, my stick-to-it-ness and my (slight) addiction to perfection has served and will continue to serve me through my battle. If I have learned anything from this crisis, it's that all we can ever do to prepare for disasters is make a solid plan and lean into it. This period of introspection and transition was necessary for my recovery, but also for me to be a vulnerable, appreciative creature who loves with her whole heart.

I admire my sister. She loves her family with her whole heart. She's anything but perfect, but that's life. And, by the way, who is? From a young age she knew what she wanted and she went for it. No regrets! She is as prepared as anyone for a disaster, but I guess that comes at a cost. She's different from me.

I am called Safe Stace. It is a nickname I've carried with me since my twenties, because I'm always focused on remaining prepared. Be that as it may, surviving my stroke taught me that it is not the things we plan for that bite us in the ass. I check that the front door is locked several times per evening. I make sure the oven is turned off before I can go to sleep. I always check on my children before I go to bed. Why? Because those are things that I can control. To some it might sound crazy, and perhaps it is.

By the same token, I need and want to remember the days leading up to and just following my stroke. Everything fades. My sister gave me that very advice when we had our first children. Everything is a phase. I don't want to let it go just yet. The minute that you let the feeling go, it is as if you're closing the door on your grief.

So I hesitate—not because I didn't think I would make it or not because I don't think I deserve it. It's simply because I have never had to face something so vast, so raw, and so bitter as death before. Facing my own mortality has changed all that is me.

# CHAPTER 14
## It's Going to be a Long Haul
*After: Battered, but decidedly unbroken.*

Until 2019, February had been a month of celebrations. All my children's birthdays take place then–we welcomed our newborn twins on Valentine's Day in 2008 and the Squidge on the twenty-eighth of 2012. My mother-in-law shares the twins' birthday and my father-in-law celebrates his on the nineteenth.

My late grandfather's birthday, who was, by the way, a wily and crazy-like-a-fox kind of guy, was cause for even more celebration. He was, and is, deeply connected to me, in a father-like role. That's why 20 February, his birthday, seems like an unlikely day to change my life forever. This is the day I suffered my stroke, as a result of a carotid artery dissection.

I recall only bits of that day. Bits which I hang on to, like a lifeline. It is still too painful for me to let that feeling of nothingness, of intoxication, go.

I remember the fear in Johan's voice when he came into our bedroom. Like a drunk, I let it go. Or Katja in our bedroom demanding that I say something sensible. It felt as if she was lovingly swaddling me with a cashmere duvet. It was peaceful. In no way did I feel rushed or hurried.

I learned on that day that the acceptance of death is alluring. It's not scary in itself. That's precisely why it is so damn scary. I could have slipped out of my life so very easily. No thoughts about Johan. No last-minute tips for my three children. Just peacefully parted.

What am I expected to feel? If I'm being honest, I've taken the time to feel everything and anything. I mourned the loss of my handwriting, of my ability to quip, of doing simple arithmetic, of setting the supper table without having to count and recount the places, of being able to run down the stairs, of not being afraid each time someone is kicking a ball near to me, of not having to ask a friend if my damn nose has snot on it.

I'm sick of dealing with the effects of this motherfucking stroke.

I have allowed myself the time and space that my stroke deserves. It most definitely deserves the power to influence decisions and affect change. It forced its will on me. I couldn't stop it. It *is* me.

My experience with surviving this messy, sometimes awful, yet very purposeful, medical crisis means that I am flummoxed, perplexed, and at a loss daily.

I suffered a multitude of set-backs. Including non-fluent aphasia, agraphia, emotional regulation disorder, impaired cognitive functions, sensory integration disorder, and right-sided hemiparesis. To date, I have spent the better part of my time working on my recovery.

Some days, I do it well. I meditate. I visualize. I treat everyone with respect. It's all a part of the bright, new, sunny side of my stroke-survivor-ness. On other, darker days, I really get it wrong. The demons creep up on me and paint my world black. As I write this, it is with hope in my heart. I hope that with each passing day, the pain becomes smaller in my mind and less significant in my soul, leaving me with yet another cause for celebration.

I, personally, am a shameless self-advocate for me. I talk about my stroke. I support others in their fight to get better. And I disagree vociferously with anyone who puts a label on recovery. Recovery is personal. Recovery should detail explicitly your wants, needs and wishes. Recovery doesn't just mean that you are alive. Unless it does.

We, as survivors, have been given a fluke shot at defining what our 2.0 looks like. We reserve the right to figure that out by combing through all the shattered pieces of our lives, keeping some and tossing others aside. We also reserve the right to change our minds. As many times as necessary.

It's too hard to follow along with this recovery nonsense unless it affects you. I get it. Of course it's easier to greet me on the street with a casual, "Hi! How are you," instead of "Hey, how's your recovery going?" I not only get it, but after my first year of recovery, I asked myself: how would I treat someone in my position?

I'll never forget the first time I saw Johan's friend after she suffered the loss of her husband. It was at a birthday party for a mutual friend, and there she stood, surrounded by her close girlfriends. I walked up and asked her how it was going. To this day, her reply still haunts me.

She said, "My husband just died. How do you think I'm doing?" As I slunk off with shame, I vowed to never make that mistake again. You see, I wasn't unaware of her situation. I wasn't being whimsical. In my mind and my heart, I wanted her to know that if there was anything I could do to relieve her suffering, I would most certainly do it. She just needed to say the word! However, that message probably didn't come across in my casual, flippant question.

I was talking about this issue with my husband. He said that it's hard on him, as well. Right after my stroke, he had a deluge of supporters sending him their thoughts and messages of love and strength. Today, however, unless you have gone through something similar, things may seem "normal;" you might think he is, or I am, okay.

I think that as long as you show up, you can never be faulted. I've been on both sides. It's tricky to get it right. As long as you act with integrity and don't say hurtful things, you're doing all right.

I spent an inordinate amount of time collecting stories of my fellow stroke survivors and relating to them with interest and wonderment. Little by little I began to unravel a thread. Something was crystallizing in my mind about people and, more specifically, the people who I've gotten to know more intimately through, and because of, my stroke.

I began to formulate a theory about the people who you surround yourself with during a life-changing event. The doctors, family, friends, and other people you meet along the way generally tend to flow into one of three categories: the superfluous, the skeptics and, my favorite, the sparkly people.

I had a hard time, in the months following my stroke, letting go of all the things that were competing for space in my brain. All of the projects, all of the social activities, all of the needs and wants of anyone other than myself were ending up in the back seat. It's not that I wanted to be anti-social, so why was I pushing people away?

It was just then that I realized that I wasn't rejecting them, I just couldn't keep up with them and all of their stories and chatter. I no longer had the energy to follow along with these superfluous people in my life. Aside from my family and my therapists, I had limited room for anybody else in my close circle. Maybe it sounds unfriendly, but I had to give myself permission to focus my power and my spirit on myself. Through no fault of their own, those extraneous people actually fell by the wayside at that point in my life.

Then there are the skeptics who are not prepared to give you, or your disabilities, a sideways glance. That's okay, unless you need them. I've been to several doctors, neurosurgeons and orthopedics, a myriad of healers and several physiotherapists for my chronic Babinski reflex. I found only two who took me seriously. The others just sat back, barely hiding their condescension. They just didn't understand.

There are also people like my child's teacher, who dismissed me and my concerns like he was flicking off a gnat from his arm. They are poisonous, filling my head with doubts and causing me deep pain at the same time. It is simple to say that these people are not worth my time. I know it. You know it. And yet, my stomach just turns in knots at the thought of dealing with them.

That's why I regularly choose to focus on sparkly people. Mirka, Gabby, Kenny, Kim, Elisabeth, Sara, Bex, Amanda, Fiona, Tina, Nancy, Shona, and Kara: I feel profoundly touched by our friendships. They are sparkling, and more than that, they make me sparkle as well.

All along this journey, I have to believe that our sparkly people find us, lift us up, and lavish us with the incredible gift of their spirit. I am not actively looking for a sparkly person to enter into my life, but on the same hand I'm open and willing to accept them.

As human beings who want to grow, it is incumbent on us to allow a person to flow between the superfluous, the skeptics and the sparkly people. Until my stroke, I didn't always understand this. I was particularly shut down and would vehemently shut you out if you trampled on my heart. I've said it many times, but this stroke seems like a gift in this particular way.

The ability to let the people in my life weave their way in and out, at their own pace and to the beat of their own drums, makes perfect sense. Johan once told me that he pictures the people in his life as if they are living in the same apartment building, and he is the boss, living on the penthouse level. If his mate makes him angry, he can send him to the basement. But, if he does one good thing, he can work his way back up to the first floor. And to the second. All the way until they're partying with him at the penthouse once again. I get that now.

With time, I hope to gain the energy to allow more people into my life again, to include more in my inner circle. As well, I will genuinely appreciate how much glitter the sparkly people bring into my life, without holding a grudge if they slip.

I'm learning to accept those people who have trod on my heart without punishing them. I've let misdeeds go without reacting to them externally. In my mind, of course, I still need to have a conversation with myself. It takes time to process. More often than not, I manage to see the other person's side and I just kick them down a level in my townhouse. I stop to consider the offense without automatically throwing them into the dungeon.

What I'm anxious about, if I'm truly honest with you, is how I'm dealing with the skeptics, those who have made my life harder than it should be. I find this one more challenging than the rest. If you're relying on someone, if you've made a deal with them, I find it an inexplicable burden to accept it if they abandon the commitment.

Take the physiotherapist who spoke Japanese in front of me and on my behalf. Did he think that he was solving anything for me? Do I care? I still have him regulated to the basement... one step above the dungeon.

Truth be told, I have had trouble finding peace with my cynics. With my disciplined practice of gratitude, I hope that these instances become fewer and fewer. All I can ask of myself is that I do the work to let myself heal. In the space of love, I have to believe that anything is possible.

Let's walk the path, my path, of what it means to be beyond recovered, of me finding my 2.0. A neurosurgeon once said to me that my "speech ability had improved considerably and daily conversation has been realized." What he did not see is that I have mastered the art of compensatory strategies. For instance, to buy time, I clear my throat when I can't find the correct word. I quickly ask questions, to force my companion to talk. I have memorized a few words that work in many situations. What that neurosurgeon also didn't see was when my stress levels go up, or when I am tired, my ability to communicate plummets. Can he rightfully say that he's accurately assessed my abilities?

He made a faulty judgment based on his goals for me and decided on his own that I had achieved them. He didn't ask me whether I agreed.

When I sit down to write a blog, an email or even just a simple text message, what you don't see is that my word finding ability is low, my spelling is horrendous, and my fingers have their own misguided, birdbrained will. So, yes, my daily speech ability has "improved considerably." But, no, I vehemently disagree that daily conversation has been realized. I am just a smart cookie who has mastered the art of faking it until I make it.

Equally exasperating, I remember meeting Cleo's friend's mother in the park. We were talking about my journey, as she was involved with another stroke survivor's rehabilitation. She proceeded to shame and nullify me and my own rehab by insensitively commenting that, "She (the woman that she was helping) suffered a much worse stroke than you. She still cannot speak after sixteen years." Now, this is an irresponsible, foolish statement on so many levels. How dare she!? I'm not in the habit of comparing my suffering with someone else's and it feels dismissive of all the work that I've done to get to this place. I reserve the right to determine what it means to me to be successful.

When I am beyond recovered, I would like to think that it will take me a few hours to write a blog, instead of the whopping twenty hours that it took me to write my very first post, post-stroke. And that I can write it all by myself.

When I consider myself beyond recovered, then stammering in mid-conversation will simply be because there are too many words coming to my mind and I want to choose the perfect one.

When I'm perfectly recovered, I would like to think that my marriage will be stronger from having endured this calamity. I would like to believe that we, as a couple, have weathered this storm and even grew stronger. Most importantly, I can imagine us coming out on the other side as two oldies, sitting on our front porch laughing about that time when the only word which I could speak was *one*.

We are rebuilding our lives and it's crucial that we see the potential that was bestowed upon us. Potential to take the broken bits, even those that were already broken, and piece them, with the utmost care, back together again.

I will consider myself rehabilitated when I can act as my children's mother, without hesitation, when I fully trust my instincts and my intuitions. I can only imagine not having to second guess myself again and again when I pick a fight on their behalf without asking Johan.

To me, beyond recovered means that I can enjoy the process and the journey of not being truly recovered. The truth is we are always morphing, constantly progressing. I want to relish this fact. I don't want to know the questions or the answers! I want to figure them both out along the way.

For me, beyond recovered means that days may go by without me thinking about my stroke. Instead of having to hold the handrail, I might bounce down the steps lickety-split or finally feel the loose change or the keys when they are in my right pocket.

Beyond recovered means that I'd be more fluid in my thinking, that I don't see everything in black or white, and that I could easily refocus my attention when I'm interrupted.

What do I feel now? Am I terrified? There are days when the demons get to me, demons I cannot control. And on those days I just have to push through, saying, "Excuse me demons, this my life, if you don't mind." Except on the very dark days, when I succumb to the beasts, which have ganged up on me in unison. That happens from time to time and, when it does, I give myself a break. I light a candle, take a bath and visualize tomorrow. To push too hard doesn't make sense.

Am I positively overwhelmed with the amount of work I have to do? Hell yeah. Some days I just want to pull the covers over my head, instead of thinking of all the things, all the therapies, I have to go through that day. Even today, it's a struggle. Most people don't know how hard we survivors have to work. Don't give up! Take a beat and try again tomorrow.

Am I completely motivated to kick this stroke's ass? Yes, of course, don't you know me by now?

Am I mad? Now that's a great question. Never once have I felt angry about my stroke. I have accepted it as a part of me, one that I don't understand so often, one that brings me a little bit more complication than I know what to do with; but dare I venture to say that I'm at one with it? I'm not only not mad about it, but I'm giving myself the chance to learn from it. In the end, I believe I will become a much stronger, wiser version of me.

However, I'm mad at the people, the doctors, the therapists, the friends, and the family members who expect too much or too little from us survivors. I can't help it, I am. I understand that it's unfair. I understand that that's hard for them, and for you. I don't care.

I am furious at the fact that many stroke survivors cannot advocate for themselves.

Stroke is the number three leading cause of death in the United States and the number one cause of permanent disability. I am distraught by the fact there are still people who do not know the warning signs to detect a person who's having a stroke. I should know. I was one of those who didn't know.

I believe that my stroke was a wakeup call for me and a weapon to make positive change. It left me with a feeling of "What would have happened if I didn't suffer my stroke?" and "How is it possible that I didn't do the work before?"

We survivors are culpable for defining what recovery looks like. No one else. The onus falls completely on me, as the survivor, to get up the spunk and the strength, to fight for my recovery each day.

What I expect is my will, to keep pushing, to find my new self amongst the rubble, to stay present in my mind. I expect that my sharp memories of where I started and how deeply important it was for me to find that new self won't fade. I read that a mere 10% of stroke survivors actually fully recover, which leaves me feeling heartbroken. To not regain me, in all of my chaotic brilliance, to not be able to find my 2.0 whatever she looks like, brings me to tears.

I realized that the only limits put on my recovery are the ones I put there myself. I pick my exhausted self up, though battered, though not better but decidedly unbroken, one more time because I deserve a whole life. I also realized that it's ok not to know the definition of my 2.0, the finished me. At the beginning of my recovery, I thought that I knew what rehabilitation meant. I could run them off like a list: write my blogs, walk properly, perform simple maths in my head, put my contacts in, make my own decisions, make Thanksgiving dinner, travel… but now, after a full year of surviving this vicious stroke, caused by a tiny tear in my redundant carotid artery, I understand the acute difference between recovery and transformation.

Finding the heartbeat of my new self will take time. Because it has to be authentic, true to me, I have to develop this new heartbeat one step at a time, reserving the right to do it my way. As a pit bull warrior, I'm dealing with the social, the emotional and health related obstacles, for which no one is prepared, as well as the life-changing, hellish and costly effects of surviving.

I believe that we all deserve to lead the life that we want to live.

# AFTERWORD

I found the first year relentless. Because, as we would later find out, life does tend to go on. While Johan and I were stuck in a fiery pit of desolation, a bottomless and never-ending process of reading and signing forms, finding a nurse who spoke English and navigating the hospital system in a completely foreign language, we felt fully immersed in the darkness of our struggles.

However, not once did I feel the burden of this crashing down around me.

To My Family: you are one of the bravest, absolutely invincible and most bad-ass families ever. You not only took care of me when I was at my most vulnerable, you show me every day how to be strong.

To My Husband, Johan: I've said many times that I would like to write a love letter to you, Jo, for all that you've been through and all that you will go through due to my stroke. The endless doctors' appointments. The insurmountable paperwork. The ability to logically understand what has happened, but feeling helpless to banish the fears and what if's. The end of a dream. You, as the primary caregiver, have an exceptionally hard task and one you didn't ask for. *We'll make it, hon. I'll meet you on that porch swing one day. You bring the red and I'll bring the white.*

To My Children: Even though you are suffering, even if you've lost your way and your dream of everything a mother should be, you've shown an amazing gift of resilience. As small children, you have been put in a tricky spot, one which you shouldn't ever have to be in. Apart from wobbles here and there, you have a knack for focusing on the here and now and not what should be. Although it used to be me taking care of you, the dynamic suddenly shifted. You have become unintended, but not unwilling, cheerleaders.

*Lulu Belle, my onion, you are kind and wise beyond your years. I haven't forgotten our plans to visit Paris. And you're going to rock it! Friso Biso, how do you always know what I'm thinking? Amazing. Follow your heart, my pickle. You are unstoppable. Squidge, Cleo, you are all that's good in this world. And you smell like puppies in the sunshine. Yum.*

To My Mother: You are the world's kindest human, mixed with sauciness and grit. You know what it's like to struggle and climb your way back into the light. You've taught me to love in the face of defeat and to never let go of my dreams. *Here's to all that we've lost, may we never forget how we've overcome. You are my light.*

To Marshall: You were the quiet force behind my mother at this time. *I am eternally grateful.*

To Aunt Gail: One of the most thoughtful things I experienced through this time was your strong determination to make sure that Gram always could maintain her connection with me. *I will always be thankful to you that I didn't lose my grandmother in the stroke-midst.*

To Marlene & Peter: You are the strongest in-laws ever, determined to be rocklike and steadfast through it all. You've supported me in my weakest moments, giving advice and sending packages laden with love. I wouldn't be this far without you. *Thank you for enveloping me in your love.*

To Marieke: Every time I think of you, I think of strong, Fort Knox level of security. That's how you make me feel. Like nothing can get to me when you're around. I trust you with all of my being. *Darling (can I say that?!), thank you.*

To my Village: I am a Bradford county-born country girl, although I haven't lived in the country or in Pennsylvania in nearly thirty years. When my stroke struck it was in the center of Tokyo where I was living as an expat with my husband and our three children. Survival meant that our lives were torn inside out and upside down.

There are plenty of people, my village as I like to call them, who have deeply contributed to my recovery thus far. They say that it takes a tragedy to learn who your friends are. While I have found this to be true, I would add that, in life-changing moments, you also form friendships. Here are some of the kindest, most giving souls I have ever had the pleasure to meet and form relationships with.

To Katja, a no-bull-s%#t kind of a girl: Katja, you are the one I turn to as a compass and it is you that keeps me on the straight and narrow, telling me the truth when it's not convenient. You push me in ways that I find uncomfortable. It takes quite a friend to move you through these miserable bits… and to see your true potential. *Woman, I'll be your Grace any day.*

To the ultimate cheerleader, Kara, my guaca-migo: To date, I have saved every clipping, every email, every text message, every package that you've sent me since my stroke. Although the years have passed and you have even managed to visit, I (and my children) still receive those packages. You manage to love me even when I am at my unlovable worst. You see through me… to the heart of me… It's you that I try to emulate as a friend and as a kind-hearted, fully engaged Stacie 2.0. *Kara Mia, let's recreate our first trip together, shall we?*

To Maria: There are no words to say, my dear friend. We were supposed to fight together, challenge each other and grow old together. I'll forever keep the promises that I made to you. *I love you with all of my heart.*

To my dear Mirka. You had the strength to watch over Cleo on the night of my surgery. For that I will always thank you.

To my beautiful friend, Gordana: We are forever connected with the tomodachi link. I will always treasure that and you.

To my ultimate sparkly people: Michelle, Gabby, Kenny, Kim, Sara, Bex, Amanda, Fiona, Tina, Nancy, Lorraine, Shona, Annette; keep the fire lit and may you always make others sparkle from your fire.

And my strokies, Wendy, Elisabeth, Debbie & Maureen: Keep on fighting the good fight. You are all awesome warriors and I consider myself lucky to be a part of your *club!*

I read a statistic that around one in 15 adults in the United States are carers. It makes me shudder. On my one year stroke anniversary, we gathered as many of my villagers as I could, into one room as a celebration, commemorating my first year. It only struck me when I gazed across the room how precious the gift of giving yourself truly is. These people have lives of their own. Have families of their own. Still, they chose to be here, celebrating my life.

Friendships are minted when tragedy strikes. Caring for me was not a choice. It just fell from the clear blue sky

# ACKNOWLEDGEMENTS

I put off writing this part until the very end, because how do I thank the village who challenged me and pushed me further along the arduous, precarious, slope of recovery? Or those creative and talented souls who showed me great patience throughout the making of this book? Danny, my insightful and shrewd editor. Eva, my brilliantly smart cover designer. And, Claire, who cleverly and wholeheartedly gave my words their voice.

While there are many people to whom I owe a debt of gratitude, there's one person who, more than any other, guided me through this incredible journey and helped make this book possible.

I'll always remember meeting Seth Koster, the week after surviving my stroke. At the time I could not speak. In fact, I could only mutter one word, which was "One". My husband and I sat on my hospital bed and talked virtually with Seth, who was in Vietnam, about him working with me as my Speech Therapist. My cheeky husband told Seth that I was a writer and I was livid with him! I was suffering from aphasia, agraphia and countless cognitive issues that made writing seem impossible. I couldn't imagine myself writing my name, let alone a book! Seth didn't blink an eye.

I liked that about him.

So, with Seth at my side, we dug in — working two hours a day, seven days a week. Two years, and a hell of a lot of work later, we had finished my first book. You see, Seth is not like any other therapists - ever. He got to the heart of what makes me tick. I admitted to him in the early days that it was my dream to write a book. We broke that down into manageable pieces that I diligently worked on with Seth by my side.

Seth, you've somehow held on (and held my head above water) these last years.

From two words in an hour's session (how boring that must have been for you!) to the insurmountable techniques we've had to learn together (I'm really sorry about the proposal!), we've forged an unlikely friendship that goes deeper than I could write on paper.

Part speech therapist and part psychologist, my brain-injured comrade, I am truly grateful for you. You've shown me how to hold on to hope. You are a true friend, Seth Koster.

There is not enough Seth in this world.

# ABOUT THE AUTHOR

Stacie Broek is a Pennsylvania country girl, who grew up riding snowmobiles and playing kick-the-can in the dewy grass with the neighborhood children. She moved to New York as soon as she could, drawn by a fascination with big city life.

Ten years and one Dutch husband later, Stacie and her husband made their home in London—which she annoyingly found NY's little sister, then Zürich—where she became a mother, and after that, Tokyo—the Switzerland of the East, where Stacie survived a stroke that left her bed-bound and speechless. The doctors told her husband that she would never write again.

One book and three half-marathons later, Stacie Broek currently lives in Zürich with her husband, Johan, and their three rockstar children; Lulu, Friso and Cleo (the Squidge).

Website: www.staciebroek.com
Instagram: staciebroek
Facebook: staciebroek

Printed in Great Britain
by Amazon